FIFTY PLACES TO DIVE

BEFORE YOU DIE

FIFTY PLACES TO

DIVE

BEFORE YOU DIE

Diving Experts Share
the World's Greatest Destinations

Chris Santella

—

FOREWORD BY ETHAN GORDON

STEWART, TABORI & CHANG | NEW YORK

Published in 2008 by Stewart, Tabori & Chang
An imprint of ABRAMS

Text copyright © 2008 by Chris Santella

Photograph credits: Pages 2, 58, 124, 140, 144, and 160: © Eric Hanauer, ehanauer.com;
pages 10, 74, and 192: © Ethan Gordon, ethangordon.com; pages 12, 24, 42, 64, 68,
98, 120, 132, and 216: © Stephen Frink, stephenfrink.com; page 16: © Norbert Wu,
norbertwuproductions.com; pages 20, 30, 54, and 176: © David Doubilet; pages 38, 78,
86, 180, 212, and 220: © Marty Snyderman, martysnyderman.com; page 46:
© Tom Phillipp; page 50, 90, 106, and 128: © Jonathan Bird, jonathanbird.net;
page 94: © Roger Munns, scubazoo.com; page 114: © Al Hornsby; page 136:
© Ivo Kocherscheidt, ivokphoto.com; page 152: © Nicolas Reynard/Getty Images, Inc.;
page 156: © Dee Scarr; page 164: © Matthew Oldfield, scubazoo.com; page 168:
© Paul M. Hudy, nc-wreckdiving.com; pages 186 and 198: © Jason Isley, scubazoo.com;
page 206: © Masa Ushioda/Stephen Frink Collection

Library of Congress Cataloging-in-Publication Data
Santella, Chris.
Fifty places to dive before you die : diving experts share the world's greatest
destinations / by Chris Santella.
p. cm.
ISBN 978-1-58479-710-4
1. Diving—Guidebooks. 2. Ocean travel—Guidebooks. I. Title.
GV837.S277 2008
797.2'3—dc22   2008001968

Editor: Jennifer Levesque
Designer: Paul Wagner
Production Manager: Jacquie Poirier

The text of this book was composed in Interstate,
ITC Tiepolo, and Scala typefaces

Printed and bound in China
10 9 8 7 6

Stewart, Tabori & Chang books are available at special discounts when
purchased in quantity for premiums and promotions as well as fundraising or
educational use. Special editions can also be created to specification. For
details, contact specialsales@abramsbooks.com or the address below.

ABRAMS
THE ART OF BOOKS SINCE 1949
115 West 18th Street
New York, NY 10011
www.abramsbooks.com

Contents

Acknowledgments 8 / Foreword 9 / Introduction 11

THE DESTINATIONS

(1) **Antarctica: McMurdo Sound** 17
RECOMMENDED BY LINDA KUHNZ

(2) **Australia: Eagle Hawk Neck** 21
RECOMMENDED BY KAREN GOWLETT-HOLMES

(3) **Australia: Great Barrier Reef** 25
RECOMMENDED BY MIKE BALL

(4) **Australia: Lord Howe Island** 29
RECOMMENDED BY TAS DOUGLASS

(5) **Bahamas: Grand Bahama** 33
RECOMMENDED BY JIM ABERNETHY

(6) **Belize: Gladden Spit** 37
RECOMMENDED BY MIKE BECK

(7) **British Columbia: Browning Pass** 43
RECOMMENDED BY JEFFREY L. ROTMAN

(8) **California: Channel Islands** 47
RECOMMENDED BY TOM PHILLIPP

(9) **Costa Rica: Cocos Island** 51
RECOMMENDED BY MARTHA WATKINS GILKES

(10) **Cuba: Jardines de la Reina** 55
RECOMMENDED BY FILIPPO INVERNIZZI

(11) **Ecuador: Galápagos** 59
RECOMMENDED BY ERIC HANAUER

(12) **Fiji: Bligh Water** 63
RECOMMENDED BY STEVE WEBSTER

(13) **Florida: Key Largo** 67
RECOMMENDED BY STEPHEN FRINK

(14) **French Polynesia: Rangiroa** 71
RECOMMENDED BY PAUL SLOAN

15 Grenada: Island of Grenada 75
RECOMMENDED BY ETHAN GORDON

16 Hawaii: Kona 79
RECOMMENDED BY MARTY SNYDERMAN

17 Honduras: Utila 82
RECOMMENDED BY ADAM LAVERTY

18 Indonesia: Komodo National Park 85
RECOMMENDED BY GREG HEIGHES

19 Indonesia: Lembeh Straits 91
RECOMMENDED BY CHUCK NICKLIN

20 Indonesia: Nusa Lembongan 95
RECOMMENDED BY ROGER MUNNS

21 Indonesia: Raja Ampat 99
RECOMMENDED BY BERKLEY WHITE

22 Indonesia: Wakatobi National Park 103
RECOMMENDED BY KEN KNEZICK

23 Maine: Passamaquoddy Bay 107
RECOMMENDED BY JONATHAN BIRD

24 Malaysia: Layang Layang 111
RECOMMENDED BY SIMON CHRISTOPHER

25 Malaysia: Sipadan 115
RECOMMENDED BY AL HORNSBY

26 Republic of Maldives: Maldives 119
RECOMMENDED BY DUANE SILVERSTEIN

27 Republic of the Marshall Islands: Bikini Atoll 123
RECOMMENDED BY DOUG TOTH

28 Mexico: Akumal 127
RECOMMENDED BY ROXANNE PENNINGTON

29 Mexico: Isla Guadalupe 131
RECOMMENDED BY PATRIC DOUGLAS

30 Mexico: Santa Rosalia 135
RECOMMENDED BY SCOTT CASSELL

31 Mexico: Socorro Island 141
RECOMMENDED BY MARK TALKOVIC

32 Micronesia: Truk Lagoon 145
RECOMMENDED BY CLIFF HORTON

33 Mozambique: Inhambane 148
RECOMMENDED BY SHELDON HEY

34 Myanmar: Mergui Archipelago 151
RECOMMENDED BY INGO SIEWERT

35 Netherlands Antilles: Bonaire 155
RECOMMENDED BY DEE SCARR

36 New Zealand: Doubtful Sound 159
RECOMMENDED BY AMY WEST

37 New Zealand: Poor Knights Islands 163
RECOMMENDED BY MATTHEW OLDFIELD

38 North Carolina: Cape Hatteras 167
RECOMMENDED BY DAVE SOMMERS

39 Ontario: Fathom Five National Park 171
RECOMMENDED BY DAN ORR

40 Republic of Palau: Palau 175
RECOMMENDED BY WAYNE HASSON

41 Papua New Guinea: Milne Bay 181
RECOMMENDED BY STAN WATERMAN

42 Philippines: Malapascua Island 185
RECOMMENDED BY ANDREA AGARWAL

43 Scotland: Scapa Flow 189
RECOMMENDED BY KIERAN HATTON

44 Republic of Seychelles: Mahe 193
RECOMMENDED BY DEBBIE SMITH

45 South Africa: Aliwal Shoal/Waterfall Bluff 197
RECOMMENDED BY SIMON ENDERBY AND JASON ISLEY

46 Sudan: Sha'ab Rumi 203
RECOMMENDED BY DOMINIQUE SUMIAN

47 Kingdom of Tonga: Vava'u 207
RECOMMENDED BY PAUL STONE

48 United Kingdom: Grand Cayman 211
RECOMMENDED BY SERGIO CONI

49 United Kingdom: Grand Turk 217
RECOMMENDED BY MITCH ROLLING

50 Washington: Puget Sound 221
RECOMMENDED BY JANNA NICHOLS

ACKNOWLEDGMENTS

This book would not have been possible without the assistance of the expert divers who shared their time and experiences to help bring these fifty great venues to life. To these men and women, I offer the most heartfelt thanks. I would especially like to thank Ethan Gordon, Tom Phillipp, and the Scubazoo crew, who made many introductions on my behalf and helped educate me on the fine points of their beloved underwater world. I also want to acknowledge the fine efforts of my editor Jennifer Levesque, designer Paul Wagner, and copyeditor Sylvia Karchmar, who were all instrumental in bringing this book into being. Also thanks to Claire Greenspan, whose untiring work has helped make the Fifty Places series viable. Thanks also go to my agent Stephanie Kip Rostan, for her sage counsel and equalizing influence. I also want to thank my mom and dad, who comforted me after an ill-fated diving outing in Acapulco in 1977, and encouraged me to pursue my dream of being a writer. Most of all, I extend the deepest thanks to my wife, Deidre, and daughters, Cassidy Rose and Annabel Blossom, who have displayed tremendous patience, flexibility, and love. I hope that some of the wonders of the underwater world will be intact when they're old enough to take to the sea.

FOREWORD

"What is your favorite place to dive?": a reasonable question frequently posed to me when I am dripping wet and half naked, usually as I am peeling out of my wet suit along with a boatload of divers doing the same. It is typically during this not-so-sexy strip tease that the post-dive euphoria peaks and people's minds spin wildly ahead to answer a basic question, "What dive destination could possibly be better than the one I am at right now?" As a photojournalist who specializes in photographing and writing about dive destinations from around the world, it would seem reasonable for me to be able to weigh in on this. However, there is no simple answer.

Most every destination has something great to offer: whether it is a pristine coral reef or a luxurious hotel with convenience of diving. I know this may sound like a stock line from a travel brochure, but it is true. Sometimes the diving at a particular destination would rate average as far as the underwater world is concerned, but the personalities of the locals, the dive guide, or your fellow divers make that trip one of your most memorable. Other times the topside accommodations may feel more like rundown army barracks, but the diving is so off-the-charts incredible, that you just don't care.

Regardless, these inquiring divers don't want to hear my "politically correct" response. They want to know where they should be headed next, and so I am hard pressed to answer. It is at times like these that I steal a quote from quarterback Tom Brady, who when asked which of his Super Bowl rings is his favorite, answers, "The next one." Fortunately, author Chris Santella did not have the luxury of being so glib when creating the book *Fifty Places to Dive Before You Die*.

To write the book, Chris tracked down 50 experts from around the world to weigh in on the world's best, from British Columbia to Raja Ampat. For avid divers, this book will help you plan adventures for the rest of your life; for those who've been there and done that, the wonderful photos will remind you of the great adventures you've had! So, the next time you find yourself dripping wet and half naked on the back of a dive boat wondering what could possibly top the dive you just did: First, dry yourself off. Next, put on some clothes (or at least some sunblock). Then, pick up this book and start planning your next trip.

—ETHAN GORDON

INTRODUCTION

The earth's oceans hold many wondrous surprises—be they the small, colorful "critters" that abound in the muck off the coast of Papua New Guinea, opportunistic red demon squid haunting the depths of the Sea of Cortez, or naval wrecks testifying to conflicts past in the lagoon of the Bikini Atoll. With the advent of modern scuba equipment, more and more people are experiencing these underwater wonders firsthand. New animals, new reefs, new diving hot spots are constantly being discovered, and ardent divers long to see these destinations for themselves.

For these people, I was inspired to write *Fifty Places to Dive Before You Die*.

"What makes a destination a place you have to dive before you die?" you might ask. The presence of sharks, mantas, and other charismatic species? Incredibly rich biomass and biodiversity? Healthy reefs? A rewarding ambiance on the live-aboard or adjoining land? The answer would be all of the above, and an abundance of other criteria. One thing I knew when I began this project—I was *NOT* the person to assemble this list. So I followed a recipe that served me well in my first four *Fifty Places* books—to seek the advice of some professionals. To write *Fifty Places to Dive Before You Die*, I interviewed a host of people closely connected with the diving world and asked them to share some of their favorite experiences. These experts range from filmmakers (like Stan Waterman) to photographers (like Stephen Frink and Ethan Gordon), to marine biologists (like Mike Beck), to equipment manufacturers (like Doug Toth), dive safety advocates (like Dan Orr), and adventurers (like Scott Cassell). Some spoke of venues that are near and dear to their hearts, places where they've built their professional reputations; others spoke of places they've only visited once but that made a profound impression. People appreciate diving for many different reasons, and this range of attraction is evidenced here. (To give a sense of the breadth of the interviewees' diving backgrounds, a bio of each individual is included after each essay.)

While this book features fifty great diving experiences, it by no means attempts to rank the places discussed, or the quality of the experiences afforded there. Such ranking is, of course, largely subjective—an adventure to swim with great white sharks might prove anathema for someone with a fondness for macro life! In this spirit, venues are listed alphabetically by state or country.

In the hope that a few readers might embark on their own adventures, I have provided brief "If You Go" information at the end of each chapter, including the names of reputable dive shops and dive travel companies that serve the regions discussed. The "If You Go" information is by no means a comprehensive list, but should give would-be travelers a starting point for planning their trips. (Please note: For land-based dive venues, I have listed both lodging and dive shop information. For venues that are visited via live-aboards or from isolated resorts, I have listed only accommodations information.)

One needn't travel to the ends of the earth to have a rewarding diving experience. Yet a trip to a dream venue can create memories for a lifetime. It's my hope that this little book will inspire you to embark on some new diving adventures of your own.

OPPOSITE
This superb manta ray is deserving of an entourage— both remoras and photographer!

The Destinations

MCMURDO SOUND

RECOMMENDED BY **Linda Kuhnz**

There's cold-water diving. There's icy-cold-water diving.

And then there's Antarctic ice diving!

When she was affiliated with Moss Landing Marine Laboratories, Linda Kuhnz had an opportunity to accompany a diving research expedition to McMurdo Sound on the southern tip of Ross Island in Antarctica. "I knew for a year in advance that I'd be going, and had plenty of time to get prepped and think about the upcoming experience," Linda began. "I'd done a lot of cold-water diving with wet suits of varying thickness, but it became clear pretty quickly that I'd have to learn to dive with a dry suit. I thought that ice diving might feel confining or claustrophobic, and wasn't sure how I'd react. Some people who'd had the experience told me that when you drop down the ice hole—sometimes as much as ten feet deep—it can be a bit frightening."

Antarctica is not one of the world's most welcoming places. This is evidenced by the fact that there are no indigenous people on the continent, despite the fact that Antarctica encompasses more than 14,000,000 square miles, roughly one-and-a-half times the size of the United States! A contingent of 5,000 scientists from the twenty-seven nations that are signatories of the Antarctic Treaty maintain a year-round presence on the continent; another 25,000 or so tourists visit the warmest areas (on the Antarctic peninsula) each season. A great majority of the land mass—an estimated 98 percent—consists of ice and snow that has an average thickness of 7,000 feet; scientists believe that up to 70 percent of the world's fresh water is contained here. During the winter months, when temperatures hover in the balmy range of –40 to –90 degrees Fahrenheit, sea water surrounding the continent freezes up to 200 miles offshore, covering an area even larger than Antarctica's landmass. In the summer (December through March), the freeze recedes, though not so much as to preclude

OPPOSITE
Penguins and
marine mammals
in McMurdo
Sound are more
likely to be
encountered above
water than below.

ice diving. McMurdo Sound rests roughly 850 miles north of the South Pole, on the far western edge of the continent (or 2,400 miles due south of Christchurch, New Zealand).

According to research assembled by Peter Brueggeman of the Scripps Institution of Oceanography library, the first dive below the ice of Antarctica occurred in 1902, when Willy Heinrich, a carpenter on the German craft the *Gauss,* descended to conduct repairs. Now as then, ice diving presents several unique challenges. First among them is breaking through the ice. This task is generally achieved with a large ice auger, which is brought out to the pro-spective diving site on a tracked vehicle (imagine a very large snowmobile). Holes can be quite large, up to twelve feet in diameter; if one is extremely fortunate, the hole may be con-tained within a heated ice house, rather like an ice fisherman's shack. (Ice divers will also sometimes borrow the air holes of Weddell seals to gain purchase.) Once in the water—which can be as cold as 28 degrees Fahrenheit—you must keep warm. Dry suits are essen-tial, and it's recommended that visitors log a number of drysuit dives before arriving. You'll also want attached dry gloves, layers of polypropylene undergarments, and a regulator that's low-temperature–ready. (Fortunately for researchers, McMurdo Station maintains a well-stocked inventory of cold-water diving accessories.)

"As I prepared for my first dive, I had a mix of fun-anticipation and anxiety—it's hard not to wonder if you're going to be able to do it or not," Linda continued. "It was a bright, sunny day. I dropped down through the ice and looked up. The sunlight was coming through the ice, making it a glacier blue, one of the most beautiful things I've ever seen. I was awe-struck by how colorful it was. Just talking about it, I get chills. It was a surreal world, as beautiful as any tropical reef." Properly outfitted, Linda managed to stay comfortable. "A tiny bit of my face was exposed, the area underneath my mask where my hood comes to my chin. But overall, being cold was not a huge problem."

Visibility in the waters under the ice of McMurdo Sound can be astounding. "The water had hardly any suspended particles," Linda explained. "When you look up, you can see the ice hole very clearly, even from sixty or seventy feet. Some of my fellow researchers have been there in the early spring before there's been much sun, and hence very little plank-ton. They say that at that time, visibility can be up to 1,000 feet; one time, they drilled sep-arate holes 1,000 feet apart, and the divers insist they could see each of these exit points." Visibility of 300 to 600 feet is more common.

The kaleidoscopic refractions of light filtering through McMurdo Sound's thick ice are not its only attraction. A host of invertebrates awaits. "One of the things that I really like to

18

do is look at small stuff—perhaps because I spend a lot of time looking through a microscope in my work," Linda continued. "There's an animal called *Glyptonotus antarcticus* that's found in the waters of McMurdo Sound. In other parts of the world, this type of isopod grows to only a few centimeters. In Antarctica, I saw them up to five or six inches in length. Animals in these constantly freezing cold waters don't have to spend a lot of energy adjusting to temperature changes, and this helps them grow very large. This is true for sponges, sea stars, and other crustaceans, too. On one dive, when we went down deeper than usual—to 160 or 170 feet—we photographed sponges that were six feet tall!"

Seemingly infinite populations of krill in the waters of Antarctica provide a biomass foundation that supports vast quantities of bird, pinniped, and cetacean life. However, visitors are more likely to come upon seals and penguins on open water or above the ice than below. One local pinniped that divers would do well to avoid is the leopard seal, which frequents pack ice during the more clement months. This predator, identified by its slightly reptilian head and a white throat that's decorated with black spots, is the only seal that will attack and devour other seals.

LINDA KUHNZ is a senior research technician at the Monterey Bay Aquarium Research Institute, where she studies ecological relationships among small animals that live in the top few inches of marine sediments (infauna), and larger invertebrates and fishes that live on the sea floor or just above it. When she's not working, she's often found diving with Abreojos Diving Adventures, a diving club she operates from bases in Monterey, California, and the North Kohala coast of Hawaii.

IF YOU GO

➤ **Getting There**: Those not accompanying a research expedition will have to travel to Antarctica by boat, as no commercial air service is available.

➤ **Best Time to Visit**: Trips to the Antarctic are limited to the spring and summer—roughly November through April.

➤ **Accommodations**: The number of ships offering dive-oriented expeditions to Antarctica is limited. One operator is Australia-based Aurora Expeditions (+61 29-252-1033; www.aurora expeditions.com.au).

EAGLE HAWK NECK

RECOMMENDED BY **Karen Gowlett-Holmes**

In the popular imagination, Tasmania summons up pictures of the peripatetic Tasmanian devil, a short-lived Looney Tunes animated cartoon character. If divers had it their way, it would conjure up pictures of weedy sea dragons and the other attractions of the waters found off Tasman Peninsula.

Tasmania is a large island located 125 miles south of Melbourne, across Bass Strait. This Australian state boasts large tracts of undisturbed land; nearly 40 percent of Tasmania's 26,000 square miles is given over to national parks and World Heritage sites. It's cooler, moister, and lusher than the bigger island to the north. In addition to the Tasmanian devil (yes, there really is such a creature, a carnivorous marsupial the size of a smallish dog), Tasmania has many endemic species of flora and fauna found nowhere else. This level of endemism and diversity extends to Tasmania's marine environment, which is worlds away from the tropical environs of the Great Barrier Reef. "Our marine flora and fauna is extremely diverse for a cool, temperate environment," said Karen Gowlett-Holmes. "Tasmania is regarded as having the highest species diversity of invertebrates and algae of any temperate area in the world. It is estimated that only about 30 percent of the marine invertebrates have been formally described scientifically. Our endemic species—either to southern Australia or just southeastern Tasmania—include weedy sea dragons and hand-fish (related to anglerfish and frogfish). These creatures attract many divers to the region."

The Tasman and Forestier peninsulas are but an hour southwest of Hobart by car, yet capture all the beauty and wildness of "the island off the island," as Tasmania is sometimes called. The heavily forested cliffs, which rise 1,000 feet from the ocean, are quite spectacular to behold, either from the many hiking trails or from the water. Eagle Hawk Neck rests at the juncture of the two peninsulas. To the east rests the Tasman Sea; to the west, the more

OPPOSITE

Weedy sea dragons are closely related to sea horses, and are one of the prime diving appeals of Tasmania.

21

sheltered waters of Norfolk Bay. Most of the region's better-known dive sites are seaside. One facet of the Tasman diving experience most visitors want to experience is the giant kelp forests. Vast stands of *Macrocysti pyrifera*—ranging from twenty to 175 feet in length—were once common up and down the Tasman and Forestier peninsulas. Regrettably, the forests are in deep decline—over 90 percent have disappeared in the last ten years due to climate change. The forests in Fortescue Bay, midway down the Tasman Peninsula, are still thriving. Here, the kelp can grow some eighty feet from the sandy bottom to the surface. Divers pausing at different levels of the kelp will find a number of creatures, including cuttlefish, cowfish, banded stingarees, octopus, and one of Tasmania's underwater stars, weedy sea dragons. Weedy sea dragons are closely related to sea horses, and take their name from the leaflike extensions on their heads and bodies that provide camouflage as they move amongst the kelp and weed beds that they call home; if they're not in motion, they can be easily missed!

"Diving with the weedy sea dragons is one of the most popular activities for visitors," Karen continued. "We have several sites where there is a very good chance of seeing them. Visitors are amazed at their general appearance and also at their size—fifteen to eighteen inches—as most people expect them to be quite small. If approached carefully, they will ignore divers and continue feeding or just cruising around. In summer, most of the males will be carrying eggs." Weedy sea dragon range is limited to southern Australian waters, from Geraldton in the west to Sydney in the east, and south to lower Tasmania. Males, incidentally, carry the females' eggs on their tails—from 100 to 300—for approximately two months, fertilizing them along the way.

Devil's Kitchen and Tasman Arch are among the Tasman Peninsula's most notable above-water attractions, and the theme of artful rock formations continues underwater at Waterfall Bay. "The caves and walls at Waterfall Bay are incredibly diverse, with colorful invertebrates—including many nudibranchs—decorating the walls," Karen continued. "Cathedral Cave is the largest, and leads back into many smaller caverns with narrow tunnels and passages, often with large schools of fish near the entrances. The canyons near Paterson's Arch also offer a variety of invertebrate life and some excellent swim-throughs."

No visit to Eagle Hawk Neck would be complete without a visit to Hippolyte Rocks, a mile or so off the entrance to Fortescue Bay. The larger of the rocks supports a colony of a hundred Australian fur seals that are often ready to play. Australian fur seals are the biggest member of the fur seal family, with the largest animals approaching 1,000 pounds;

their range is typically from south Australia to Tasmania. When it comes to swimming with marine mammals, dolphins and whales often steal the limelight, but the pinnipeds at Hippolyte give the cetaceans a run for their money. "The fur seals are very curious creatures, and will often approach divers," Karen added. "Younger seals especially like to play. They seem to enjoy the divers' bubbles."

KAREN GOWLETT-HOLMES is co-owner of the Eaglehawk Dive Centre (www.eaglehawkdive. com.au) in Tasmania. She's been an active diver for more than thirty years, and works part-time as a marine biologist for CSIRO Marine and Atmospheric Research. Karen is a member of the Australian Institute of Professional Photographers (Master of Photography). She was highly commended in the British Gas Wildlife Photographic Competition for her work and was runner-up in the biomedical and scientific division of the Australian Photographer of the Year Competition 2000 and 2001. Karen was also nominated for a Eureka Award for scientific journalism in 2001. She is a certified divemaster, TDI gas blender, commercial diver, and DAN oxygen provider.

IF YOU GO

➤ **Getting There**: The Tasmanian capital of Hobart has regular service from Sydney and Melbourne through Qantaslink, Virgin, Jetstar, and Regional Express.

➤ **Best Time to Visit**: April through August is considered prime time, though diving is available year round.

➤ **Accommodations**: Eaglehawk Dive Center (+61 36-250-3566; www.eaglehawkdive.com. au) has bunkhouse-style accommodations on site, and Lufra Hotel (+61 36-250-3262; www. lufrahotel.com) offers more elegant lodging. Discover Tasmania (www.discovertasmania. com) has a comprehensive list of accommodations.

➤ **Dive Shops/Guides**: There are several dive shops around Eagle Hawk Neck, including Eaglehawk Dive Center (+61 36-250-3566; www.eaglehawkdive.com.au) and Go Dive (+61 36-231-9749; www.godivetassie.com).

GREAT BARRIER REEF

RECOMMENDED BY **Mike Ball**

OPPOSITE
At Cod Hole,
resident potato cod
seem eager
to "buddy up" with
visiting divers.

Mike Ball's primary school report read something like this: "His antiestablishment attitude may be his undoing. His attitude makes a mockery of pursuing external examinations." Like many seeming misfits dwelling in England, Mike departed for Australia. "I got to Sydney in 1969 and bought an old bomb of a car for fifty pounds and drove toward the north. When I got to Townsville, the car broke down. I had just enough money left to buy a few tanks and begin to build up a diving business. Some would say I've been broken down in North Queensland ever since!"

If you happen to enjoy diving, that's not a bad thing.

For many, the Great Barrier Reef is the very definition of exotic diving. Stretching some 1,500 miles off the northeastern tip of Australia (the province of Queensland) in the Coral Sea, it is the world's largest coral reef system. The region is home to 400 species of coral, 1,500 species of fish, seventeen species of sea snakes, six species of turtle—and the statistical milestones go on and on. The attractions of the reef for visitors are not lost on Aussies; some two million tourists visit each year, pumping an estimated $5.1 billion (AU) into the Queensland economy. While there are day-trip dives available from the cites of Townsville and Cairns, the best diving opportunities are upon live-aboard boats that travel farther afield. Mike put it this way: "Queensland and the Great Barrier Reef are quite far from most places. If people have traveled this far to go diving, I wouldn't want to just show them the Cairns basin."

With 130,000 square miles of diving habitat to choose from, it is rather difficult to paint a comprehensive picture of the opportunities the Great Barrier Reef affords. However, Mike was happy to share a few favorite dives, beginning in the south. "There's a wreck about forty-five miles off Townsville called the *Yongala*. It's quite a big ship—more than 300 feet long, and it's in relatively shallow water, 100 feet to the sea bed. As it emerges out of the gloom, it almost looks like a reef. The concentration of marine life along the wreck is remarkable. It's basically a composite of all the creatures you're going to see if you were to spend a week on the Great Barrier Reef—bloody big batfish, bull rays, sea snakes, giant trevally, Maori wrasse, huge Queensland grouper (ever-present under the bow and stern, and reaching lengths of eight feet!), sea turtles, and off the wreck, bull sharks. If you had only one day to spend diving in Queensland, the *Yongala* would be your best bet."

Thanks to the crowds and what he considers to be somewhat lower quality opportunities in the Cairns basin ("crowds" and "lower quality" are relative terms), Mike would bypass this region and push farther north to the Ribbon Reefs. The Ribbon Reefs chain extends fifty-five miles, from east of Lizard Island in the north to east of Cooktown in the south. Most of the Ribbon Reefs chain falls within the boundaries of the Great Barrier Reef Marine Park, established to protect the reef's wonders from the potential ravages of commercial fishing and other man-created havoc. "The Ribbon Reefs are on the edge of the Continental Shelf," Mike continued, "and offer the best visibility in these parts. Lots of baitfish are brought in with the currents, and that brings in trevally, barracuda, and other big fish.

"There are a number of exciting dive spots in the Ribbon Reefs. Challenger Bay is one of the most pristine spots. It's very shallow, but exquisitely beautiful, between the corals and the tropical fish. It's not a deep dive, but many internationally renowned photographers have been happy lying there on the sand and shooting what's around them. On many trips we'll do a night dive at Challenger Bay. During these dives, we'll see moray eels, lionfish, and a large barracuda that's a regular visitor. We've named him Baza. Baza has figured out that divers use underwater lights at night, and that these can be handy for hunting. If you're holding your torch in your right hand in Challenger Bay, you might find Baza hovering over your right shoulder. Then there's one swoop and gulp, and it's good night for an unlucky baitfish."

Just north of Challenger Bay is one of the reef's most venerated dive sites, Cod Hole. It takes its name from its outsize resident potato cod, which can grow to "diver-size" and beyond (some specimens reach sizes of over six feet and 300 pounds). Potato cod take their name from the spud-shape markings on their skin. "What makes the experience at Cod Hole unique is the comfort level the fish have with divers," Mike explained. "Normally when you see pictures of divers and big fish, if they're not already swimming away, the fish's body language suggests that it's feeling twitchy and getting ready to go. That wariness is how big fish have gotten big. The fish at Cod Hole have become acclimated to divers over the years. They seem happy to buddy up with you. Swimming closely with fish so big in water so clear is a special phenomenon."

Most expeditions that Mike's company leads will include a trip farther out into the Coral Sea, to Shark Reef and Osprey Reef. "It's about seventy-five nautical miles out, and the water has tremendous visibility, which is a great draw for visitors," Mike continued. "Where the top end of the Ribbon Reefs has more species variety, the reefs farther out in the Coral Sea have bigger marine life. We'll often see sizable groups of gray reef and white-tip reef sharks, manta rays, and sometimes hammerheads off the deep walls, which extend to depths of more than 3,000 feet."

For those who enjoy encounters with even bigger species, there's Lighthouse Bommie (a *bommie* is a coral-covered pinnacle), home each June and July to large groups of migrating dwarf minke whales. Minke whales are members of the baleen whale family, and are distributed throughout the world. Dwarf minkes, which reach roughly 20 feet in length and weights of five to six tons, are a subspecies limited to the Southern Hemisphere. Nearly 200 individual whales have been recorded in the northern Great Barrier Reef area in the summer. "Thanks to the dwarf minke's affinity for boats and people, divers have a chance for prolific and extended swims with these whales, more than anywhere else in the world," Mike said. (Such "swim with the whale" dives are regulated by the Great Barrier Reef Marine Park Authority.) "Guests who've had the chance to dive or snorkel with orcas and humpbacks have told me that the experience with the minkes is much richer, as these whales are naturally inquisitive. They'll come to you and try to buddy up; usually it's the other way around."

MIKE BALL is the founder and proprietor of Mike Ball Dive Expeditions (www.mikeball. com), one of Australia's main diving companies, leading trips throughout the Great Barrier Reef Marine Park and Coral Sea. He's widely recognized as a pioneer in the field. From his humble arrival in Townsville back in 1969, Mike put live-aboard diving in Australia on the international dive map. He developed a unique style of luxury, twin-hull expeditionary live-aboard to explore the distant reefs of the Great Barrier Reef and Papua New Guinea. Mike has received many accolades in his 38-plus-year diving career, including the Queensland Tourism Award for Best Tour Operator (1992) and induction into the International Scuba Diving Hall of Fame in 2004. His previous operation of eighty-five crew operating four live-aboards and a state-of-the-art diver training center has been "right-sized" to just one vessel, his favorite *Spoilsport*, so Mike can now focus on his underwater photography.

IF YOU GO

➤ **Getting There**: Most overseas visitors will fly into Cairns, which is served by a number of carriers, including Quantas, American, and United.

➤ **Best Time to Visit**: Visibility is quite good year round. The rainiest months are December through April, though the water is warmest at these times.

➤ **Accommodations**: While day trips to less remote reef sites are possible, a live-aboard gives you the greatest flexibility. Many options are available. Mike Ball Dive Expeditions (888 -MIKEBALL; www.mikeballdive.com) has been leading trips as long as anyone. Tropical North Queensland (866-582-4909; www.tropicalnorthqueensland.com.au) lists land-based lodgings options.

➤ **Dive Shops/Guides**: There are scores of dive companies serving the Great Barrier Reef region. Dive the Reef (800-207-2453; www.divethereef.com) provides an excellent overview of operators.

LORD HOWE ISLAND

RECOMMENDED BY **Tas Douglass**

Lord Howe Island is a small outpost some 373 miles east of the Australian mainland, a two-hour flight from Sydney, and a fifty-year jump back to a simpler and perhaps happier time. "Lord Howe is exceptionally clean and friendly, the kind of place where people don't lock their houses," said Tas Douglass, whose family has island roots that go back six generations. "The water is exceptionally clean and pristine, too. We're blessed with a great mix of fish life and corals—indeed, the reef is the most southerly coral reef in the world. The waters around Lord Howe are certainly uncrowded. Most people don't seem to know about the island, perhaps because of its isolation and the fact that only 400 visitors are allowed here at a time. Historically, most islanders avoided the water. It wasn't until eighty years ago that local people even swam here, let alone dove, though many people fished. Now, diving is quite popular with residents and visitors alike."

Crescent-shaped Lord Howe Island is a remnant of a seven-million-year-old volcano, and an above-water fragment of a submerged continent that geologists refer to as Zealandia. It was never part of continental Australia and thus developed an ecosystem unto itself: a mix of temperate and tropical influences, with many endemic plant and insect species. The island's volcanic past is evidenced by the two basalt mountains, Mount Lidgbird and Gower, which stand watch from the island's south end. Much of the rest of Lord Howe—roughly six square miles—is given over to forest, including the *Howea*, an endemic palm tree. In recognition of its natural beauty and unique ecosystems above the water and below, Lord Howe (and its surrounding islands) was listed as a World Heritage site in 1982; its waters are also recognized as a national marine park.

Lord Howe offers divers great diversity in terms of both the number and type of sites available. The coral reefs surrounding the island offer many dives of modest depths where

29

moorish idols, spotted sweetlips, angelfish, and moon wrasse, among other reef fish, are commonly encountered, as well as various trevally—and in some gullies, Lord Howe moray eels. The coral itself is an attraction, with some ninety varieties recorded thus far. For less seasoned divers, there's excellent terrain in the lagoon itself. Within fifteen minutes of Tas's shop, there are a number of other rich sites. The Admiralty Islands are certainly a highlight, with more than thirty dives, and consistently excellent visibility, sometimes topping 125 feet. "Tenth of June Bombora is a must-do dive at Admiralty Islands," Tas continued. "You'll find some rarities here, including green jobfish and Japanese boarfish. Another of my favorites here is called North Rock Deep. There are a lot of crayfish (rock lobster) here, and many nudibranchs. As you make your way through some of the swim-throughs, you may encounter a six-foot-long black cod that frequents the area. There are lovely yellow soft corals, and even some black-coral trees."

If there's a pinnacle to the Lord Howe Island diving experience—literally and figuratively—it's a visit to Ball's Pyramid, the world's tallest sea stack. Named for Admiral Henry Lidgbird Ball (who discovered the island complex in 1788, but named it for Richard Howe, then First Lord of the Admiralty for the Royal Navy), monolithic Ball's Pyramid rises more than 1,800 feet from the surface, an imposing stack of black basalt. The attractions below the surface are equally impressive. "It's about an hour's run—twelve miles—out to Ball's Pyramid," Tas said. "There are two little islands next to the pyramid; the islands, and the proximity to some very deep water, make for strong currents, which brings in the marine life. The pyramid is surrounded by sanctuary zones where no fishing is allowed, so the fish life is especially rich. There are some big caves you can explore; one that goes in 150 feet. There are nice walls to investigate, and some great drifts, depending on the current. It takes good buoyancy control to negotiate the drift, but it's worthwhile.

"I still vividly remember my first dive at Ball's Pyramid, at Wheatsheaf Islet. I'd anticipated going there for many years growing up, and finally I was old enough to go. The current was perfect that day to bring the fish in. We went down the anchor, and you couldn't see more than fifteen feet, there were so many fusiliers on top of the shelf where the current comes through. I didn't want to move much, as I was afraid I'd lose my dive buddy. A few minutes later, we saw a ballina angelfish—generally a very deep dweller, and once thought to be extinct—one of our specialty fish. As we were watching the wall of fish, a Galápagos whaler shark was making its way through, the fish parting in front of it, the shark turning to look at us. When we came up from that dive, no one could stop talking."

OPPOSITE
The volcanic
peaks of Lord
Howe Island
(and nearby
Ball's Pyramid)
provide a
stunning back-
drop for divers.

As mentioned above, swimming and diving are somewhat recently discovered delights for Howe Islanders, but fishing has been important for residents since the island was settled. "I fished with my dad and grandpa when I was young," Tas recalled, "and now I sometimes will dive some of the same spots that we fished. I'll bring my camera down on occasion and videotape these spots. My grandpa still thinks diving is unsafe, but he and my dad are fascinated seeing their fishing spots from the other side of the surface."

TAS DOUGLASS is the owner/operator of Pro Dive Lord Howe Island (www.prodivelord howe.com), and a sixth-generation Lord Howe Islander. Before purchasing the shop, he worked as an instructor for seven years on the island. Tas has a very strong passion for searching for new species of marine life and identifying the hundreds of species of nudibranchs around his local waters.

IF YOU GO

➤ **Getting There**: Lord Howe Island has regular service from Sydney on Qantaslink.

➤ **Best Time to Visit**: Diving is consistent September through June. July and August see strong winds that can impede travel to dive sites.

➤ **Accommodations**: The Lord Howe Visitor Center (+61 26-563-2114; www.lordhoweisland.info) lists lodgings options ranging from bed-and-breakfasts to full-service lodges. Note: only 400 visitors are allowed on the island at a given time, so reserve BEFORE showing up!

➤ **Dive Shops/Guides**: There are two dive operators on Lord Howe—Pro Dive Lord Howe (+61 26-563-2253; www.prodivelordhowe.com) and Howea Divers (+61 26-563-2290; www. howeadivers.com.au).

GRAND BAHAMA

RECOMMENDED BY **Jim Abernethy**

There are few places in the world where you can interact with large sharks all day and all night. One of those places is Little Bahama Bank, off the west side of Grand Bahama island. Grand Bahama is one of the northernmost islands of the 700-island Bahamas chain, and rests closer to Florida than any of the larger Bahamian islands. A number of the islands are flanked by banks—areas of shallower water, ten to thirty feet in depth. Many of the banks adjoin far deeper water.

"The waters around Little Bahama Bank are special for several reasons," Jim Abernethy began. "First, the region is very close to the Gulf Stream current, which is constantly pushing fresh nutrients through. Second, thanks to its location in the northern part of the Caribbean, the Bahamas have a mix of temperate and tropical water, and a wide diversity and abundance of marine life. The Bahamas have the largest conglomeration of large sharks I've ever seen—tigers, which can go up to twenty-four feet, and great hammerhead, which can reach twenty-one feet. Bull, lemon, and oceanic white tips can also be found there."

Found in temperate and tropical seas the world over, tiger sharks take their name from the stripes that ornament their sides. They average twelve to fourteen feet in size, and are known for their catholic diets, taking bony fish, turtles, crustaceans, birds, and other sharks; man-made garbage is sometimes found in their stomachs. Research suggests that these fish feed a great deal on rays, especially stingrays. They are marked by the straightness of their heads, and prominent dorsal fins that resemble the fins of a killer whale.

Like many shark divers, Jim and his team chum the water with assorted fish remains to bring the sharks in. Unlike some others, these divers are in the open water with no cages present. "We brief everyone on how to behave before we go in the water, so that the large sharks don't mistake us for their food," Jim continued, "and we have crew members in the water to insure everyone follows our rules for diver safety." When Jim is leading an excursion around Little Bahama Bank, there are several spots he's likely to hit. "We'll visit a site called Carcharias Cut, a fairly shallow reef dive of forty-five to seventy feet. It takes its name from the great white shark, as one was seen there some years back. We're not after great whites, though—here we'll generally find Caribbean reef sharks, up to twenty-five at a time. We'll also get lemon sharks, great hammerheads, and tigers here, and bull sharks in the winter months. This site's close to the Gulf Stream current, so the visibility is consistently good, sometimes over one hundred feet. There's also a huge cave that's frequented by large schools of glass minnows, and we'll often see loggerhead, hawksbill, and green turtles as well.

"Another spot we'll visit—especially if we're after tiger sharks—is called Tiger Beach. There's a shallow reef and a section with turtle grass as well. It's all very shallow—fifteen feet and less—and we'll get the sharks right up to the shore. We've had occasions where there have been twenty tiger sharks and thirty lemon sharks there, no animal less than eight feet in length. It's awe-inspiring to be in the water with these fish in such prolific numbers, especially when we know how their populations have been decimated in other parts of the world."

While sharks are the emphasis for many of Jim's excursions, it's always fun to mix things up a bit—and who better to while away some time with than the wild dolphins at White Sand Ridge. "The area is home to 150 Atlantic spotted dolphins and forty bottlenose," Jim continued. "They are completely wild, not rewarded with food for their interactions. They simply love to interact with people. Visitors come from everywhere for a chance to swim with them. We do both day and night dives. In the daytime, you have to exert yourself a bit—if you don't swim with the dolphins, they'll lose interest. But if you can dive down with them, they'll play. Keep-away is a favorite game; give them a scarf, and they'll pass it around to each other. At night, they move into deeper water in the Gulf Stream, where they'll feed on squid and flying fish. Using lights, we'll attract the squid and flying fish to the surface, and the dolphins will follow. They feed for an hour or so, and then they're ready to play. During these sessions, we've also seen sailfish, swordfish, and marlin."

Despite sharks' fearsome reputation, Jim's guests have never had an attack from any shark, despite hundreds of cageless dives. In fact, he's found that sharks can be very playful—and that some show a decided penchant for photography. "Among serious underwater photographers, there's an ongoing debate between the merits of Canon and Nikon cameras," Jim said. "I'm a Canon man myself. I mention this because we've had sharks 'borrow' cameras from photographers on twenty-five different occasions—and on two of those occasions, the sharks actually took photographs. The first, an animal we call Baby Cakes, has figured in ten of the twenty-five camera removals. On this occasion, Baby Cakes borrowed the camera—a Nikon D70—from a Spanish biologist. The first picture he shot was of the back of his own throat. It was out of focus, dark—overall, a terrible shot. Baby Cakes eventually spit the camera out, and we saw the strobe fire—this shot was of Tiger Beach, perfectly level and in focus. Not bad.

"The second tiger shark to have a go at photography is an animal we call Nacho. He happened to take my camera—a Canon 20D. Nacho swam off with the camera like a little kid who's just gotten a new toy; he seemed giddy. He swam around with the Canon for fifteen minutes, spitting it out, grabbing it again. He even shared it with three other sharks, who also played with it. After fifteen minutes, I was getting a little concerned; after all, it's a seven-thousand-dollar camera! As a few of us pursued Nacho, we saw the strobes firing—one, two, three, four shots—and then he let go. When we reviewed the pictures, we saw that he'd taken three horizontal shots and one vertical. As any photographer knows, cover (vertical) shots pay better than inside shots, so we figured that the sharks were learning. Like most of us, they started with a Nikon and then progressed to the superior system, Canon. You can clearly see the images getting better as well. Of course they all chose the digital cameras. And some people still think they are dumb!"

JIM ABERNETHY is the owner of Scuba Adventures (www.scuba-adventures.com), which leads diving excursions out of Palm Beach, Florida, and the Bahamas. When he started snorkeling in the bathtub, his parents took him to the ocean, at the ripe old age of five; he hasn't gotten out of the water since. Certified at the age of twelve, Jim has been diving for more than thirty years, and has worked in the dive industry as a captain, scuba instructor, and dive boat operator since 1981. An accomplished photographer and videographer, his footage has been seen on BBC Wildlife, Discovery Channel, National Geographic, Animal Planet, CNN, and many local Florida stations. He has a passion for sharks, turtles, dolphins, and manatees, and works diligently with numerous agencies to protect them. When he's not leading trips, Jim enjoys flying in the *Over-Sea'r*, his amazing flying inflatable boat. He also enjoys spotting mantas, dolphins, sharks, turtles, and anything else of interest to divers from his own spotter plane, while guests dive from his boats.

IF YOU GO

➤ **Getting There**: Freeport, one of the main cities of the Bahamas, is on Grand Bahama island, and is served by many major carriers. Some of the live-aboards that visit Little Bahama Bank depart from the Palm Beach area.

➤ **Best Time to Visit**: Jim Abernethy leads trips between December and April, prime time for shark viewing.

➤ **Accommodations**: Jim Abernethy's Scuba Adventures (888-901-3483; www.scuba-adventures.com) leads a number of live-aboard shark-oriented trips to Little Bahama Bank and beyond. The many lodging options on Grand Bahama island are outlined on the Grand Bahama Island Tourism Board Website, www.grand-bahama.com.

➤ **Dive Shops/Guides**: If you opt to stay on Grand Bahama, there are a number of dive shops that lead trips, including UNEXSO (242-373-1244; www.unexso.com).

GLADDEN SPIT

RECOMMENDED BY **Mike Beck**

When "diving" and "Belize" are mentioned in the same sentence, it's generally images of the Blue Hole and Shark-Ray Alley that spring to mind. But for a few weeks each spring, attention shifts to the waters off Placencia and an area called Gladden Spit. For it is here that snappers, groupers, and other reef fish gather en masse to spawn—and where whale sharks appear in large numbers to partake of the bounty.

"All the diving I've done in Belize has been in the southern part of the country," Mike Beck began. "While the reef diving is decent, I wouldn't describe it as spectacular. But when you're there in April or May and there's a full moon, you're in for quite a treat."

Belize is a small Central American country blessed with a very large reef. Formerly known as British Honduras, Belize is tucked on the southeastern quadrant of the Yucatán peninsula between the Quintana Roo province of Mexico to the north, Guatemala and Honduras to the west and south, and the western extremes of the Caribbean to the east. With much of its original rainforest intact, Belize has become a favored ecotourism destination in recent years for birders and those hoping to catch a glimpse of a jaguar, as the big cats still thrive here. Divers have long known Belize for the attractions of the Meso-American Barrier Reef, which stretches over 400 miles along the entire Belizean coast, north to Quintana Roo, and south to parts of Guatemala and Honduras. It's the longest barrier reef in the Western Hemisphere, and the second longest in the world. Gladden Spit Marine Reserve encompasses a portion of the reef directly east of the Placencia Peninsula, which lies 100 miles south of Belize City.

Regrettably, the Meso-American Barrier Reef is one of the world's most threatened reefs, suffering degradation related to water temperature and quality changes, habitat destruction, and unsustainable fishing. It's just possible that the mating/feeding melee at

Gladden Spit could point conservationists in Belize and beyond toward a model that might retard reef and fish deterioration—at least a small bit.

As early as March—but more reliably April and May—large schools of dog and mutton snappers (and somewhat smaller collections of groupers) congregate around Gladden Spit to spawn. Their eggs, milt, and larvae are planktonic in nature, and these tiny morsels attract the attention of significant concentrations of the fish world's largest plankton eaters—whale sharks. (No one knows how far whale sharks travel to partake of the feast, though by the sheer number of fish, one would conjecture that they travel from many points in the Caribbean.) The whale sharks aren't the only party that takes notice of the aggregation. The snappers are good-eating fish, and local fisherman, armed with nets, were hard-pressed not to take advantage of the easy angling the large balls of snappers represent. The harvesting of the snappers as they tried to reproduce had a devastating impact on future fish populations. Enter the World Wildlife Fund, the Nature Conservancy, and a local environmental group called Friends of Nature. First the WWF worked with Friends of Nature to conduct the research necessary to gain Gladden Spit its marine reserve status. Next, the TNC worked with Friends of Nature to provide local fishermen with an alternative to unsustainable snapper harvesting—training and certification as dive and sport-fishing guides. Studies have shown that fishermen can earn more money from the mating bacchanalia by showing visitors the proceedings rather than netting the fish. Left mostly undisturbed, the fish stocks have much better odds of long-term survival.

Is the snapper aggregation along Gladden Spit worth all the hoopla? Mike Beck's description of the scene would suggest a resounding "Yes!"

"The dive operator we used (Seahorse Dive Shop) had a pretty good idea where we'd find the fish aggregations," Mike continued, "and we sailed to a likely spot and spent most of the day lounging around, waiting for the big event. As the sun began to set, we got in the water. Pretty soon, we could see snappers and groupers running along the outer edge of the reef, about 180 feet out. They'd streak along, then ball up and release their eggs and milt. Suddenly, the water was a boiling, milky white. When you're in the water as this occurs, you feel as though things are spinning. As the milky substance disperses through the water, the whale sharks rise out of the depths to feed on the spawn. Sometimes, even if the spawn isn't on, you can blow bubbles with your regulator and the sharks will come up. It seems so incongruous, these massive beasts right next to you, eating these tiny bits of egg and milt.

OPPOSITE

Whale sharks arrive at Gladden Spit each spring to gorge on snapper eggs and milt.

"I was down with the snappers on one occasion when the whale sharks had come up, and I heard the sound of dolphins clicking. I turned around, and there was a whale shark cruising about ten feet below the surface, surrounded by dog snappers, with a dolphin bow-riding his wake, just off his nose."

Diving around Placencia is not limited to love-struck snappers and gorging whale sharks. The inner reef (or lagoon) boasts abundant Gorgonian corals, southern stingrays, and eagle rays in relatively shallow depths. On the exterior of the Meso-American Great Barrier Reef (where the drop-off reaches depths of nearly 3,000 feet), one may encounter bigger animals—turtles, tarpon, and mantas, among them. After his experience at Gladden Spit, Mike Beck opted for a more relaxed outing. "There's a group called TIDE (Toledo Institute for Development), that helps arrange eco-oriented tours in southern Belize with local residents. I'd heard they could connect me with someone who could give me a taste of life on the water as locals experience it. I ended up out in a panga with an old-timer. We did a little snorkeling, a little hand-line fishing, and then went to some sea-grass beds to collect conch. The fellow runs a little restaurant out of his house. We took what we'd gathered back there and he made us dinner."

MIKE BECK is a senior scientist with the Marine Initiative of the Nature Conservancy (www.nature.org) and a research associate at the University of California Santa Cruz. His current research for the Nature Conservancy focuses on two areas: (1) marine ecoregional planning and (2) marine policy. Mike has either led or been a team member on plans for the northern Gulf of Mexico; Cook Inlet, Alaska; Puget Sound and Georgia Straits, Washington and British Columbia; Southern California; southeast Atlantic (North Carolina, South Carolina, Georgia, Florida); Greater and Lesser Antilles. He holds a Ph.D. from Florida State University (Tallahassee), and an M.S. and B.A. from the University of Virginia (Charlottesville).

IF YOU GO

➤ **Getting There**: Placencia is reached via Belize City on Tropic Air (800-422-3435; www. tropicair.com) and Maya Air (501-223-1140; www.mayaairways.com). Belize City is served by American (via Miami) and Continental Airlines (via Houston).

➤ **Best Time to Visit**: Local dive shops lead spawning/whale shark dives from March through June, though April and May are most consistent whale shark producing times.

➤ **Accommodations**: The Placencia Tourism Website (www.placencia.com) lists lodging options for the region, ranging from *palapas* to full-service resorts.

➤ **Dive Shops/Guides**: There are a number of dive shops around Placencia. Mike had an excellent experience with Seahorse Dive Shop (501-523-3166; www.belizescuba.com).

BROWNING PASS

RECOMMENDED BY **Jeffrey L. Rotman**

The waters of British Columbia hold a special place among cold-water diving aficionados. And among B.C. devotees, Browning Pass—and particularly God's Pocket rank near the top of the "must dive" lists. This is certainly the case for photographer Jeffrey Rotman. "The waters here are the very definition of a rich marine environment," Jeffrey ventured. "It seems like there are animals on top of animals in every available space. Part of the problem I face when diving there is trying to decide what to photograph first."

OPPOSITE
An Irish lord,
one of the denizens
of the cold, clear
waters around
God's Pocket.

Browning Pass is situated off the northeastern tip of Vancouver Island, near the town of Port Hardy, and some 300 miles north of Victoria at the island's southern tip. The open waters of Queen Charlotte Sound lie just to the north, and the strong currents that charge through Browning Pass sustain a vibrant assembly of fish and invertebrate life. The currents can make for some challenging conditions, and some spots can only be accessed during slack tides. Several islands, including Hurst, Bell, and Boyle, dot the pass, providing more sheltered sites. God's Pocket references both a provincial marine park and one of these sites, a relatively shallow (fifteen- to forty-five-foot) cove on Hurst Island that can be easily accessed from the dock of one of the region's dive destinations, God's Pocket Resort.

"God's Pocket gives you an abundance of wonderful, close-up macro life," Jeffrey continued. "There are decorator crabs that are so well camouflaged that they can't be photographed. There are all sorts of other crabs (including Puget Sound king crabs), and huge starfish—big as beach balls, with twenty-four arms, and very fast moving. These starfish are so large that they actually eat other starfish. As far as I'm concerned, it's the nudibranch capital of the world, with some giant nudibranchs reaching a foot in length. All the invertebrates grow incredibly large, thanks to all the nutrients that the current cycles through."

Invertebrate life can grow quite large around Browning Pass and God's Pocket. "One of the big stars of God's Pocket is the giant Pacific octopus," Jeffrey said. "In this area, they can grow to one hundred pounds in four years. At God's Pocket, you can sometimes observe them feeding along the bottom." This cephalopod is the largest of the known octopus species; around Browning Pass, their arms can reach lengths of up to six feet (with a combined reach of twelve feet) and a maximum weight of 150 pounds. Each arm has 280 highly sensitive suckers, which assist the creature in hunting. Giant Pacific octopus generally feed on bivalves and crabs, though they've been observed to eat larger, more nimble creatures, including small sharks and birds.

The second big star of the Browning Pass region is the wolf eel, sometimes known as wolf fish, the more common name for the species in the Atlantic. Though eellike in appearance, wolf eels are technically members of the blennie family. "They are utterly bizarre looking," Jeffrey continued, "with a head like a football, a body that's five or six feet long, and a mouth full of huge teeth. There are some wrecks in the waters around Browning Pass, and you'll often find the wolf eels there; they can be enticed out of their hiding places with the offer of a sea urchin." Sea mammal life is also prevalent around Browning Pass, including large numbers of humpback whales, sea lions, and sea otters. "If you're lucky, you might come upon white-sided dolphins that you can play with," Jeffrey added. Orcas are also commonly encountered here, though you're more likely to see them en route to a dive site than while you're in the water.

There are more than twenty well-regarded dive sites in the greater Port Hardy/ Browning Pass region. These include Seven Tree Island, Barry Islet, Dillon Rock, Crocker Rock (where the wreck of the freighter *Themis* lies), North Wall, and Frank's Wall. If there's one dive that encapsulates the Browning Pass experience, it's the Browning Wall; Keith and Jon, the one-name keepers of seaotter.com, have called it the "mecca of cold-water wall dives." Browning Wall reaches depths of over 200 feet, but many treats await you soon after you descend beneath the kelp that layers the surface. Swatches of soft coral in orange, pink, and red unfold alongside glove sponge, anemones, and ruffled orange-peel nudibranchs. Crevices and ledges are populated with rockfish, red Irish lords, and the occasional lingcod, with octopus making appearances, too. Macro lovers will want to train their lenses on some of the myriad small crabs that call the wall home.

The wonders below the waters of northern Vancouver Island are only enhanced by the scenic surroundings of its rugged, heavily forested coastline. Port Hardy is the farthest point north on the island that one can drive to, and its largely undeveloped environs give one a sense of what conditions must have been like here hundreds of years ago. If Port Hardy is remote, the diving lodges most visitors frequent seem worlds away. "God's Pocket and The Hideaway are a little off the grid," Jeffrey concluded. "But for the lucky few that get there, they're in for a real treat."

JEFFREY L. ROTMAN is one of the world's leading underwater photographers. He is the author of numerous books and articles on marine life and was named BBC Underwater Wildlife Photographer of the Year in 1991. He has also won the National Press Photographers Award for Picture of the Year in 1994 and 2000. He lives in New Jersey.

IF YOU GO

➤ **Getting There**: Port Hardy, at the northern end of Vancouver Island, is served by Pacific Coastal Airlines (800-663-2872; www.pacific-coastal.com). Alternatively, Port Hardy is roughly a four-hours drive north of the ferry terminal at Nanaimo.

➤ **Best Time to Visit**: The season runs from from April through October.

➤ **Accommodations**: Several dive-oriented lodges serve the Browning Pass region. These include Browning Pass Hideaway Lodge (877-725-2835; www.vancouverislanddive.com) and God's Pocket Resort (800-246-0093; www.godspocket.com).

CHANNEL ISLANDS

RECOMMENDED BY **Tom Phillipp**

The diving attractions of California's Channel Islands are many, but for Tom Phillipp, one feature stands out: the kelp forests. "Many people feel that they have a familiarity with kelp forests from viewing them from the surface," Tom began. "The brown mats viewed from above hardly do them justice. They are unbelievable underwater. From below, it's almost like you're swimming through a redwood forest. Stalks grow one hundred feet up from the bottom; when conditions are right, kelp can grow two feet a day. Golden rays of sunlight filter through the canopy. The forests are an ecosystem unto themselves. Small animals are attracted to the kelp to find food and, in turn, to hide from larger predators that come seeking them. For me, swimming through the kelp is almost a religious experience."

The Channel Islands are an archipelago of eight islands that lie off the southern coast of California. They stretch 160 miles, from San Miguel in the north (about sixty miles due west of Ventura) to San Clemente in the south (seventy miles due west of San Diego). The other islands include Anacapa, Santa Cruz, and Santa Rosa, collectively known as the Northern Islands; and San Nicolas, Santa Barbara, and Santa Catalina, the Southern Islands. The four Northern Islands, plus Santa Barbara, make up the Channel Islands National Park, a 250,000-acre nature preserve. The character of the Channels varies greatly. San Miguel is exposed to harsh, open ocean conditions, where fifty-mile-per-hour winds are common, and a rock-riddled coastline makes navigation a tricky proposition. For these reasons, San Miguel sees fewer than 300 visitors most years. On the other end of the scale, Santa Catalina (usually shortened to Catalina) sees more than one million visitors annually, largely because of its twenty-odd-mile proximity to a little town called Los Angeles, regular ferry service, and plentiful tourist attractions. Of the eight islands, only Catalina has a town—Avalon, which has a year-round population of 4,000.

OPPOSITE
The kelp forests
of the Channel
Islands are
reminiscent of
the grandeur of a
copse of redwoods.

DESTINATION

8

Giant bladder kelp (*Macrocystis pyrifera*) is a member of the seaweed family; the "bladder" refers to the polyps that children like to pop. While it can be found from Alaska to Baja California, giant bladder kelp is thickest in the southern part of its range, especially around the Channel Islands. It thrives in waters with depths from twenty to 120 feet, and temperatures below 68 degrees (low fifties are ideal). Kelp anchors itself to rocks on the sea floor with rootlike holdfasts, and spouts central stipes that reach toward the surface. Blades, each with a bladder, extend from the stipes. Kelp is harvested and processed to create algin, which is widely used as a food additive; it is even more important as a food-source platform for the many creatures that call it home, from nudibranchs, sea anemones, sea cucumbers, and mysid shrimp, to clingfish, kelpfish, and juvenile rockfish, to feeding octopus and the occasional sea lion—not to mention passing pelagics. Conditions around the Channel Islands conspire to create a perfect environment for nurturing kelp and other sea creatures. Here, an ocean upwelling circulates nutrients that sustain legions of plankton that provide a fertile base for other marine life. Combine this with the islands' location near the boundary of colder northern and warmer southern waters, and you get a high level of biodiversity that causes some to call the Channels "North America's Galápagos."

Each of the islands in the Channel system has special appeals for divers. The southernmost island, San Clemente (not to be confused with Richard Nixon's resting place, which is on the mainland), is all about variety. San Clemente boasts a wreck (the naval destroyer USS *Butler*), fine spear fishing, and Tom's favorite kelp forest (off the southern section of the island). San Nicolas and Santa Rosa are about California spiny lobsters—very big lobsters. In California, divers are permitted to take these crustaceans for their consumption from early October to mid-March. Lobster hunting is a nocturnal game; Tom's biggest catch is a creature of thirteen pounds! Catalina is the area's most popular dive site (due in part to the sheer number of visitors), and offers the Channel's best shore diving. You'll have ample opportunities to meet Garibaldi, a bright orange damselfish that serves as California's state fish. Santa Cruz has an abundance of caves and caverns for exploration, including the Painted Caves, which extend almost one-quarter mile long and stretch to widths of 100 feet, with an above-water ceiling that reaches 160 feet. Santa Barbara is home to large rookeries of California sea lions, who make for amusing dive companions. "They'll come right up and interact with you, blowing bubbles at you," Tom continued. "Pups may even chew on your fin blades. Watching how easily these wonderful creatures glide around makes you realize how unfit humans are to be underwater. We're so slow in comparison.

"People often ask me where the best diving is," Tom continued, "and when I say 'California,' people say 'But the water's so cold.' I always reply that diving in cold water is not a problem, but being cold *while* you're diving is a problem. If you take proper precautions to be warm and comfortable while diving in cold water, chances are you'll love it. The visibility can be incredible when you're a little removed from the islands. I've had guests from Hawaii who said they've never seen water so clear in all of their diving at home. I think California and the Channel Islands are pretty tough to beat. After all, where else can you swim through kelp forests, interact with pinnipeds and perhaps blue and gray whales, plus have encounters with big game fish and even find basking sharks?"

TOM PHILLIPP has worked around the diving industry for most of his adult life, as an instructor, in retail, and in dive equipment manufacturing. He is currently product manager for the Pro Dive Division of Aqualung. Tom has dived throughout the South Pacific, the Caribbean, the Mediterranean, the Sea of Cortez, and along the east and west coasts of North America.

IF YOU GO

➤ **Getting There:** The Channel Islands are accessible from anywhere in southern California, from Santa Barbara to San Diego.

➤ **Best Time to Visit:** September through December offers the best visibility, though you can dive the Channels year round.

➤ **Accommodations:** Most Channel Islands diving trips are two to three days on live-aboard boats (see below). Shore dives are available on Catalina; the town of Avalon (on Catalina) offers a broad range of lodging options, which are highlighted by the Catalina Island Chamber of Commerce (310-510-1520; www.catalinachamber.com).

➤ **Dive Shops/Guides:** For the northern Channel Islands, Tom recommends Truth Aquatics (805-962-1127; www.truthaquatics.com) in Santa Barbara. For the southern chain, he recommends Horizon Charters (858-277-7823; www.horizoncharters.com) out of San Diego.

COCOS ISLAND

RECOMMENDED BY **Martha Watkins Gilkes**

Fortune hunters have long set their sights on Cocos Island as a repository for ill-gotten treasures. Pirates, buccaneers, and other assorted ne'er-do-wells have visited the island for more than three hundred years, purportedly parking their plunder on this remote outpost off Costa Rica's Pacific coast. Some believe that the Treasure of León (Nicaragua), the Treasure of Lima (Peru), and countless shipments of gold and jewels stolen from Mexico by Spaniards (and relieved from the Spaniards by pirates) found their way to Cocos.

For Martha Watkins Gilkes and countless other divers, the true treasures of Cocos lie off its coastline. "Cocos is one of the few places I've dived where you're pretty much guaranteed action with big pelagics," Martha began. "Sometimes it's large schools of hammerheads, other times white-tip reef sharks, a giant whale shark, or even swordfish. And of course there are always the dolphins—large schools riding the bow of the boat and frolicking in the water with you—something all divers dream of."

Cocos is an uninhabited volcanic island that lies 300 miles southwest of Cabo Blanco, Costa Rica. Thanks to the isolation that made it a popular haunt for pirates, the island's ecosystems—both marine and terrestrial—have remained largely intact; for this reason, it has been designated a national park and a World Heritage Site. The large numbers of *tiburones* in the waters off Cocos have gained it the sobriquet "Island of the Sharks." (Indeed, Cocos has been immortalized in an IMAX film of that name, shot by underwater filmmakers Howard and Michele Hall; some believe that Cocos was also the model for the setting of the blockbuster novel and film *Jurassic Park*, and for Robert Louis Stevenson's *Treasure Island*!) The sharks and other pelagics are drawn to Cocos by the pinnacles surrounding the island, further remnants of its volcanic past.

If one were forced to identify one "signature" piscine attraction of Cocos, it would have

OPPOSITE
The promise of
large schools
of scalloped
hammerheads
is one of the great
attractions of
Cocos Island.

9

DESTINATION

to be the island's prodigious schools of scalloped hammerhead sharks. Scalloped hammerheads (*Sphyrna lewini*) can grow to lengths of 14 feet. Their namesake head shape is believed to aid the sharks in their quest for prey by distributing their electrolocation sensory pores across a broader surface area, and enlarging their nasal tracts. While other shark species will display schooling behavior, none school to the extent of hammerheads. (Studies conducted in the Sea of Cortez suggest that schooling behavior helps female hammerheads hover near their nocturnal feeding grounds; researchers have termed the behavior "refuging.") While no one knows exactly why the hammerheads of Cocos gather in groups of twenty, fifty, one hundred, or more, everyone agrees that watching such a school glide above you at Alcyone or Dos Amigos Grande (two reliable shark sites) is not something you'll soon forget.

The thrills of Cocos are not limited to just hammerheads and other sharks. Marbled stingrays, Pacific manta rays, and moray eels are commonly encountered there, along with large schools of horse-eyed jacks and yellow-fin tuna. Marlin and green turtles are also regularly seen. (Many species can be found at depths of sixty feet, though if you're able to go deeper, you'll likely see more.) "Diving at Cocos was the only time I've ever seen sailfish underwater," Martha continued. "We were down filming when two large specimens were suddenly swimming at us. When they noticed us in the water, they threw up their sails and turned away. It was really mind-blowing to see that; it makes me even sadder now when I come upon them mounted on the wall."

For Martha, the thrill of Cocos begins on the crossing to the island. "It's a thirty-six-hour boat crossing, and each time I've gone it's been one of the high points of the trip," she enthused. "We've seen pods of dolphins and whales each time. I've seen dolphins many times in the wild, but to have one hundred dolphins riding the bow of the ship is a magical experience." Several live-aboards—the *Okeanos Aggressor* and the *Undersea Hunter*—serve Cocos, and the program generally goes like this: "The mothership anchors in one of the island's sheltered bays," Martha continued, "either Wafer or Chatham. From there, inflatable boats take you out. There's generally one or two morning dives, one or two afternoon dives, and the option of a night dive. The night dives are really wild thanks to all of the shark activity. I recall one night dive when there was a large group of white tips nestling under the coral heads, waiting to ambush baitfish. I noticed that one of my swim fins was dangling down where the fish were coming through, and figured that I'd better pull back, or I'd become part of the feeding frenzy! On my visits, I don't do night dives every night. Most people are pretty worn out after the day's dives, as the currents are pretty strong and the emotional aspect of diving in waters like Cocos is exhausting. The adrenaline is pumping as you are filming such exciting, large marine life."

Though the diving off Cocos is certainly first-rate, visitors will want to take a few mornings or afternoons to explore the island itself. Land visits are strictly controlled by the Costa Rican government to maintain the character of the island, but with a little planning, excursions can usually be arranged. "I've come upon few places as unspoiled as Cocos," Martha added. "In nearly every bay you land, there's rainforest with exquisite waterfalls. I think that hiking up the riverbeds leading up to the waterfalls is as exciting as the diving around the shoreline." Cocos' rivers and pools are home to freshwater fish, and make for a refreshing bathing interlude. Popular land stops include the boulders at Chatham Bay, where many of the island's past visitors carved their names.

MARTHA WATKINS GILKES is the owner and operator of Fanta Sea Island Divers on the island of Antigua. She has been diving for more than thirty years and instructing for more than twenty years, and has frequently worked as an underwater model and assistant to international underwater filmmaker Stan Waterman. She is also an accomplished underwater photographer and writer, and has published *A Diving Guide to the Eastern Caribbean* (Hunter Publications) and *Shipwrecks of the Caribbean* (Macmillan Publishers). Martha has dived all over the world, including the Red Sea, South Pacific, the English Channel, and throughout the Caribbean and the Galápagos. In 1994 she was presented the Platinum Pro 5000 Hour Diver Award. In 1998, Martha was admitted as a fellow member of the Explorers Club of New York City; in 2002, she was inducted into the Women Divers Hall of Fame, where she has served as president since 2004.

IF YOU GO

➤ **Getting There**: Live-aboards depart from Punta Arenas, Costa Rica. Nearby San José is served by many carriers, including American, Continental, and Delta Airlines.
➤ **Best Time to Visit**: Prime time is May through October.
➤ **Accommodations**: There are two live-aboard options for visiting Cocos—the *Okeanos Aggressor* (800-348-2628; www.aggressor.com) and the *Undersea Hunter* (800-203-2120; www.underseahunter.com).

JARDINES DE LA REINA

RECOMMENDED BY **Filippo Invernizzi**

An unintended boon of Fidel Castro's rise to power was the barring of visitors from Los Jardines de la Reina (The Queen's Gardens), a 150-mile-long archipelago of some 250 islands located fifty miles off the southern coast of Cuba. Recognizing the region's rich marine life—and its potential for tourism—Castro's government designated the area (consisting of 1,000 square miles) a Cuban national park in 1996. Closed to commercial fishing and inhabitation, Los Jardines comprise one of the world's great protected saltwater wilderness areas—and certainly the largest protected marine park in the Caribbean. It's said that in the earlier days of the revolution, Los Jardines was Castro's favorite sport fishing grounds. In his youth, he was also a passionate diver. (The CIA apparently knew of Castro's interest in diving; there are several fairly well-documented accounts of dive-focused assassination attempts, including one involving an exploding conch shell and another, a tuberculosis-bacilli-infused regulator.)

"The proliferation of marine life in Jardines de la Reina since the national park designation has been amazing," said Filippo Invernizzi. "With the help of scientists from all over the world, an entire ecosystem, an entire chain of marine life, has been regenerated. The area preserved even encompasses the migratory passages of some species. When I started diving here before the conservation measures were put in place, it would be very common to not encounter any sharks during a dive. Now, seeing seventy or eighty sharks per dive is more the norm."

The name "Jardines de la Reina" was bestowed upon the archipelago by Christopher Columbus, who named them in honor of his patron, Queen Isabella of Spain, on his second voyage to the region in 1494. As you approach Jardines from the mainland, "garden" may not be the first descriptor that springs to mind. Topside, Jardines de le Reina is marked by

OPPOSITE
Guests are
guaranteed shark
encounters with a
variety of species
at Jardines de la
Reina, including
silky sharks.

abundant mangroves, sea grapes, and the occasional scrubby pine. Below water, however, the true gardens reveal themselves; walls festooned with brightly colored sponges and corals. The mangroves, while perhaps lacking in color, prove an excellent nursery for baitfish, which propagate and attract the bigger animals that in turn draw divers. One of the largest denizens of Jardines is the goliath grouper (formerly known in some regions as the jewfish). Individuals of 200 to 400 pounds are commonly found around the archipelago; in the Caribbean, they can reach 750 pounds and more, feeding on crustaceans, smaller fish, and even young sea turtles. Tarpon, which are a main attraction for fly fishermen who visit the area, are also here in significant numbers, reaching over six feet and one hundred pounds.

Frequent shark encounters are perhaps the main draw to Jardines de la Reina, and it never disappoints; in fact, Avalon Diving Center offers guests a money-back guarantee if they're not able to dive with sharks. Five species of sharks are found among the reefs here—silky, nurse, and Caribbean reef with great frequency, lemon and great hammerhead somewhat less frequently. "Silky sharks are the most common, and certainly the most friendly," Filippo said. "Visitors get very excited when they see the numbers of sharks we can attract, and how approachable they are. Our divemasters will sometimes stroke the silky shark's belly, which seems to calm them. At these times, guests can touch the sharks if they wish; some get so excited, they will kiss the sharks!" Whale sharks will also make an appearance around Jardines de la Reina, especially in the late summer and fall.

There are more than 120 identified dive sites around Jardines de la Reina, though Filippo said that operators tend to draw from a selection of 70 to 80 sites each month, so other areas can have a rest. (With a limit of 300 visiting divers a year and 150 miles of reef to choose from, it's not hard to dole out Jardines' treasures in small tastes!) A few celebrated sites include Black Coral One, Pius Reef, and El Farallón. Black Coral One boasts a small cave and a large coral pinnacle, and is a sure-fire spot to find reef sharks. Pius Reef is a riot of colorful sponges and gorgonian coral, and home to abundant reef fish. El Farallón features a number of swim-throughs where groups of jacks race to and fro. Silky sharks know a treat awaits when the boat appears, and are often queued up by the time divers return to the craft.

The music of the Buena Vista Social Club has sent good Cuba vibrations to the world, and those who've made the trip generally concur that one of the joys of diving Jardines is the chance to interact with the Cuban staff. "They are great characters, and are willing to go the extra mile to give guests a great experience," Filippo said. An added bonus of traveling to Jardines de la Reina is the chance to encounter a saltwater crocodile. The species found here is the American crocodile, which ranges from the Florida Keys south to Venezuela and even Peru, and east to Haiti and the Dominican Republic. They average about twelve feet in length at maturity, and can grow as large as twenty-three feet. "Before the marine park was established, the crocodiles were almost extinguished around these waters," Filippo said. "They are coming back now, but are very shy around people. We very rarely see them while we're diving, though there are places we can go where guests are virtually guaranteed to find them from above the surface." While they greatly resemble alligators in appearance, American crocodiles can be differentiated by longer, more slender snouts. They are catholic carnivores, feeding on small mammals, birds, fish, crabs, carcasses, and—given the chance—younger crocodiles. "Except for summer, the crocs will come up to the boat at night, and we'll feed them," Filippo added. "It's a nice after-dinner treat for our guests."

FILIPPO INVERNIZZI is co-founder of Avalon Outdoor, a fishing and diving center that was established in Cuba in 1993. His fly-fishing and diving operations are located in Jardines de la Reina, Isla de la Juventud, and Cayo Largo. Filippo continues to oversee marketing endeavors for the company from its offices in Mendoza, Argentina.

IF YOU GO

➤ **Prime Time**: Conditions are optimal November through April, though diving is still good through the end of the season in August.

➤ **Getting There:** North American citizens traveling to Cuba generally stage in Cancún, Mexico. Flights from Cancún to Havana are offered on Mexicana Airlines (800-380-8781; www.mexicana.com) and Cubana (888-667-1222; www.cubana.cu). From there, your outfitter will make necessary arrangements to get you to the boat. (While at press time it is still against the law for US citizens to travel to Cuba without State Department preapproval, it's estimated that 30,000 Americans travel each year to Cuba without the US government's blessing. If you go, you will be traveling at your own risk.)

➤ **Accommodations**: All diving at Jardines de la Reina is from live-aboards. Avalon Diving Center (+39 338-732 0517; www.divingincuba.com) pioneered destination diving here, and has a floating hotel (the *Tortuga*) and several live-aboards at their disposal.

GALÁPAGOS

RECOMMENDED BY **Eric Hanauer**

The word "Galápagos" conjures up many images—giant turtles, sea lions, iguanas, and, of course, the specter of a bearded Charles Darwin, scribbling furiously in a notebook. There's no reason to believe that the great British naturalist spent any time below the cool Pacific waters 600 miles off Ecuador. Had he done so, he would've likely been impressed.

OPPOSITE
Marine iguanas
are one of the
fascinating

"Before my first trip, I was anticipating the Galápagos on two levels, literally—the birds and iguanas above the water, and the assorted creatures underwater," began Eric Hanauer. "I was pleasantly surprised by the marine life I encountered. The cast of characters was familiar, similar to what I found in the Revillagijedos and around Cocos in Costa Rica. Plus there is incredible sea lion activity, and the presence of exotic endemics like penguins and marine iguanas."

creatures you're
sure to encounter
around the
Galápagos.

The first recorded mention of the nineteen islands and numerous islets that compose the Galápagos was recorded in 1535 by the bishop of Panama, Tomás de Berlanga. The islands seemed so dry and uninhabitable that he didn't bother to name them, though he did make note of the "galápago" or giant tortoise that he encountered there. For the next 300 years or so, sealers, whalers, and assorted buccaneers used the Galápagos as an occasional base of operations, slaughtering legions of sea turtles for meat. By the time Darwin arrived in 1835, the islands' only permanent human residents were members of a penal colony established by the Ecuadorian government on the island of Floreana.

Darwin had been away from his native England for nearly four years on the HMS *Beagle* by the time he reached the Galápagos, collecting specimens and observations. During the five weeks he spent on the islands in 1835, Darwin noted that while the bird and reptile life he encountered on each of the six islands he visited was quite similar, there was some variation in each species. This led him to believe that the animals had adapted over time to the microhabitats of each island. The notion of adaptation or evolution fostered at the Galápagos would be the foundation for *The Origin of Species*, which was finally published in 1859.

It is the many currents (Counter Equatorial, Humboldt, South Equatorial, and North Equatorial) that intersect around the Galápagos that have created such a diverse and unlikely assemblage of creatures. Scientists believe that the Galápagos were created from volcanic activity on the ocean floor, and that they've never been connected to a continent. All of its terrestrial residents arrived on the islands by swimming (seals, dolphins, penguins), floating (tortoises, iguanas, insects, some plants) or flying (birds, seeds floating in air currents) from as far afield as the Caribbean and the Antarctic, and the confluence of currents is the best explanation for their arrival. Once there, the animals were able to adapt and survive, thanks largely to the absence of predators, with the exception of man.

"One should note that diving is not easy at the Galápagos," Eric continued. "There's big swells, and you often have a long, bumpy boat ride to the diving site. The water can be cold, and people who have never worn anything thicker than a three-millimeter will have to adjust to the constricting feel and additional weight of a seven-millimeter wet suit. The currents are strong, and the visibility is not pristine. But the rewards of the marine life make the challenges worthwhile. After all, where else do you have the opportunity to swim with penguins, marine iguanas, and Galápagos sharks, all in the same day? It's like going back to a primeval time." (Galápagos sharks, incidentally, have a broad but spotty distribution, though they were first identified around the islands at the turn of the century.)

Diving sites in the Galápagos can be divided into two sectors: the south, where most of the islands are clustered; and the north, which means Wolf and Darwin Islands (sometimes called Wenman and Culpepper, respectively). Visitors are allowed to land on the southern islands to partake of the incredible land-based animal encounters offered there; most feel that the diving is somewhat richer around the isolated northern islands, which lie some 150 miles from Santa Cruz and San Cristóbal, Galápagos's main points of entry. Eric has experienced both. "On my first trip, we stayed in the south. I recall our encounters with schools of golden rays, Galápagos sharks, and some hammerheads. On my second and third trips, we spent more time around Wolf and Darwin. We saw vast schools of hammerheads; at Darwin, I wedged myself into the rocks at one point to anchor myself in the current, so I could watch the hammers swim overhead. The barnacles on the rocks tore up my wetsuit. We also came upon whale sharks on almost every dive." Some 400 fish species are regularly observed around the Galápagos, including manta, marbled and spotted eagle rays, moray eels, creole fish, Moorish idols, yellow-tailed surgeonfish, and king angelfish. Green turtles, marine iguanas, fur seals, and sea lions fill out the show.

It would be a shame to travel to the Galápagos and only spend time underwater. The islands' many endemic inhabitants, including land iguanas, lava lizards, Darwin's finches (thirteen species in all), and blue-footed boobies—not to overlook the world's northernmost population of penguins and the prehistoric giant tortoises—are habituated to human visitors to the point of being tame. (Island visitation is closely monitored by the Galápagos National Park to protect local fauna yet make the animals accessible to guests.) "Some people visit a diving venue only to check that place and certain species off their lists," Eric added. "They never see what's on land. I always try to include land experiences in my travels, especially at a place like the Galápagos."

While great efforts have been taken by the Ecuadorian government and the international conservation community to preserve the integrity of the Galápagos, Eric sees warning signs. "Ecuador has seen destructive fishing practices, including shark finning, which is a danger signal. Many fishing families are moving to the islands from the mainland, and they are overharvesting lobsters and sea cucumbers. There's probably too much tourism as well. I don't know how long it will be before the marine life there seriously deteriorates."

ERIC HANAUER (www.ehanauer.com) is a widely published writer and photographer specializing in the underwater world. Author of three books (*Diving Micronesia; Diving Pioneers: An Oral History of Diving in America;* and *The Egyptian Red Sea: A Diver's Guide*) as well as nearly 1,000 articles, his work has appeared in posters, magazines, books, videos, and CDs, on subjects ranging from travel to diving history, instruction to equipment. Nearly fifty years of active diving have brought a unique perspective to Eric's work. In travel writing, he covers the land as well as the underwater features of an area, from the standpoint of the local culture as well as that of the visitor. As an instructor and equipment expert, Eric writes from a background of vast experience. His oral history book reintroduced America's diving pioneers to an entire new generation. Eric is a retired professor from the Kinesiology Division at California State University, Fullerton. An aquatics specialist, he has trained more than 2,500 scuba students, and introduced the grab start to competitive swimming while coaching in the 1960s. Born in Stuttgart, Germany, and raised in Chicago, Eric was educated in the Chicago public schools, then earned a B.S. in physical education at George Williams College, and an M.S. in physical education at UCLA. Eric lives in San Diego with his wife, Karen Straus, who is also an active diver and underwater photographer.

IF YOU GO

➤ **Getting There**: Visitors generally fly to the Ecuadorian capital of Quito, and from there, fly to the Galápagos. Quito is served from Miami by LAN Ecuador, Continental, Delta, and American Airlines, among others. TAME (www.tame.com.ec) offers flights to San Cristóbal.

➤ **Best Time to Visit**: You can dive the Galápagos year round, though the high season is considered November to April, and July and August.

➤ **Accommodations**: A number of live-aboards serve the Galápagos; Galápagos Adventures (866-626-8272; www.galapagosadventures.com) outlines the many options.

BLIGH WATER

RECOMMENDED BY **Steve Webster**

It's not likely that Captain William Bligh had much of an opportunity to enjoy the tropical appeal of Fiji—let alone its underwater marvels—as he sailed around the islands in the HMS *Bounty*'s launch in 1789. After all, he was feeling a bit put out—he'd just been victim of one of history's most infamous mutinies, and was at the time under hot pursuit from two canoes full of cannibals.

Steve Webster was able to take in Fiji at a more relaxed place, though like Captain Bligh, he came to the archipelago by way of Tonga. "I had friends who had dived in the South Pacific, and I had seen many PBS programs on the topic," Steve began. "I certainly was curious. About ten years back, some friends had planned a diving trip to Tonga. At the last minute they had to cancel, and I went in their stead. It was a wonderful trip, but the emphasis in Tonga is on humpback whales. I'm more interested in coral reefs. When I mentioned this to the crew on the *Nai'a*, the live-aboard we traveled with, they encouraged me to visit Fiji. I put together a trip with volunteers from the Monterey Bay Aquarium. Since that first trip, I've been back eleven times."

The Republic of Fiji consists of some 300 islands (and a number of smaller islets) situated nearly 3,000 miles southwest of Honolulu. Only one hundred of the islands are populated, and most of Fiji's 918,000 residents live on the two largest islands, Viti Levu and Vanua Levu. Fijian waters comprise a vast area and provide many diving opportunities, but most feel that the region of central Fiji offers the best experience. The *Nai'a*—a well-respected live-aboard that operates extensively in Fiji—focuses most of its efforts around Lomaiviti, Namena, and the Bligh Water; the latter rests between Viti Levu and Vanua Levu.

"For the coral reef diving I enjoy, I haven't felt the need to look further than Fiji," Steve continued. "I cut my teeth on such diving in the Caribbean forty years ago. There's far

greater diversity in the South Pacific; where there might be seventy species of coral in the Caribbean, there are 700 in the tropical Pacific. The same is true of fish species. Fiji has also been spared the severe coral disease outbreaks that have degraded some Caribbean reef systems. Fiji is especially renowned for its colonies of soft corals. Because they lack the solid skeletons of hard corals, soft corals are flexible, and often resemble plants. You also have many bommies in the Bligh Water. They're very contained, generally no more than 100 or 200 feet across the top. The tops are lush with typical stony coral—acroporids, brain coral, and the like. The vertical walls have soft corals and sponges sticking out from them. Here you'll find clownfish, shrimp, pipefish, urchins, sponges, flatworms, and many other colorful little reef fish. I should mention that it's not all coral and other invertebrates in Fiji; while I'm interested in invertebrates, I have friends who have fish lists of Fiji with more than 1,200 species."

Cat's Meow is one of the Bligh Water's most notable bommies. Resting in waters roughly 90 feet deep, Cat's Meow is adorned with soft corals in a spectrum of colors; there's a tunnel near the foot of the bommie where divers can swim through. "Colorful zoanthids abound at Cat's Meow," Steve described, "like little colonial anemones. You'll see a lot of bowl coral, which is related to mushroom corals," Steve said. "They resemble an upside-down salad bowl—sometimes you'll see what resembles a whole field of upside-down salad bowls. They're not attached to the sea floor or the reef. When the bowl coral gets turned over by the current, it keeps growing. You get a sense of the marine world's order at a place like Cat's Meow. There are real neighborhoods. In one place on the reef, there's one species; in another place, another species. Circling around the bommie, you get schools of barracudas, jacks, occasionally tuna, hammerhead and gray reef sharks, and hawksbill turtles." Steve shared a little secret: "There's an IMAX film called *Coral Reef Adventure* that Howard and Michele Hall did. The footage is attributed to Australia, but it's really Cat's Meow and other spots in Fiji."

Steve recalled one recurring experience that seems to capture the ambiance of Cat's Meow. "Toward the end of a dive, I'll come up to a point in the water column about 15 feet from the surface," he continued. "There are often huge schools of anthias—zillions and zillions of these two-inch and three-inch fish. As I hover, the anthias are feeding on plankton, and jacks are darting in and out, grabbing anthias here and there. The anthias aren't afraid of you, as you're not darting after them. The jacks aren't interested in eating you, as you're too big. You can let yourself wash back and forth in the midst of all this, essentially

OPPOSITE
Fiji is especially renowned for its colonies of soft corals.

12

DESTINATION

becoming part of the system. You can watch the world work as long as you'd like; it's a very pleasing pastime after you've seen the moray eels and octopus and other more dramatic species."

Others may soon have the chance to become part of the system at Cat's Meow: Steve plans to set up a camera around Cat's Meow (or another nearby bommie) to capture an hour's worth of footage that will eventually become the foundation of a virtual aquarium at the Lucile Packard Children's Hospital at Stanford University.

DR. STEVE WEBSTER has been involved with the Monterey Bay Aquarium since its conception in 1976; he retired as senior marine biologist at the aquarium in 2004. Steve studied biology at Stanford and taught at Northfield Mount Hermon School, in Massachusetts, for five years. In 1965 he returned to Stanford and its Hopkins Marine Station in Pacific Grove. He received his doctorate from Stanford in 1971, when he began teaching invertebrate zoology at San Jose State University. In 1978, he left San Jose State to begin work on the Monterey Bay Aquarium as project coordinator. He was the director of education during the aquarium's first sixteen years of operation. Steve serves on the board of trustees for the York School, the Sea Studios Foundation, and the Elkhorn Slough Foundation. He has served on and is past chair of the Monterey Bay National Marine Sanctuary Advisory Council. Steve has been a diving instructor and underwater photographer for forty-five years. He is a popular speaker on natural history topics ranging from Monterey Bay to the Caribbean, the Sea of Cortez, the tropical Pacific, and the Galápagos Islands. Currently, Steve leads diving trips to Fiji once or twice each year. He has a dog named Cody and a cat named Cachagua.

IF YOU GO

➤ **Getting There**: Nadi, on the island of Viti Levu, is the main staging area for Fijian dive expeditions. It's served by Air Pacific (800-227-4446; www.airpacificusa.com).

➤ **Best Time to Visit**: April to October is the prime season, though good diving is available year round.

➤ **Accommodati**ons: Steve highly recommends the *Nai'a* (888-510-1593; www.naia.com.fj), which has been operating here since 1993.

KEY LARGO

RECOMMENDED BY **Stephen Frink**

"I showed up in Key Largo in 1978 on vacation with an M.S. in experimental psychology, a brief stint in commercial photography, and some recreational diving experience," Stephen Frink began. "I noticed that a lot of people were diving, but that they weren't taking underwater pictures—and figured that they should be. So I rolled the dice a bit and opened up a photo lab and underwater camera rentals. It turned out that there was wonderful synergy. Since Key Largo is the most northerly landmass in the Keys, it has the greatest influence from the flow of the Gulf Stream, and thus has the greatest probability of getting clear water. Thanks to its proximity to Miami, Key Largo was also the focus of early marine conservation efforts, most notably from John Pennekamp. Thanks to Pennekamp, Key Largo was protected early on, and now offers some of the best reef diving in the United States." (John Pennekamp Coral Reef State Park was designated in 1960, making it America's first undersea preserve.)

Key Largo is part of the Florida Keys National Marine Sanctuary, a 2,800-square-nautical-mile area that encompasses the archipelago of the Keys, and swatches of the bordering Atlantic Ocean, Gulf of Mexico, and Florida Bay. Thanks to the 127.5-mile Overseas Highway (the southern end of US Route 1), the Keys are America's most accessible slice of Caribbean life. Managing the sanctuary to balance the needs of commercial fishermen, assorted recreational visitors, and of course the ecosystem, which draws the first two stakeholders here, is a constant balancing act. While the two parties able to verbalize their opinions on the matter are never completely happy, marine life seems to have responded favorably. "When I take divers out around Key Largo, they are utterly incredulous at the fish populations that we have, just six miles out from land and fifty miles south of Miami," Stephen continued. "You can't find big concentrations of fish like this anywhere else in the

Caribbean. Thanks to the protections that are in place, we're allowing the prolific marine nursery of Florida Bay and the northern Keys to operate as nature intended. The result is the explosion of fish life."

In the case of Key Largo, Mother Nature has had a bit of help in the form of several prominent artificial reefs, courtesy of the sinking of the *Duane*, the *Bibb*, and the *Spiegel Grove*. The *Duane* and *Bibb* are twin 327-foot US Coast Guard cutters that were sunk in 1987, and rest at a depth of 120 feet about half a mile apart. Of the two, the *Duane* is the more sought-after attraction, due to its upright orientation, and one of the most popular dive sites around Key Largo. "The *Duane* may be the best shipwreck in this hemisphere for color and concentration of marine life," Stephen continued. "It's cloaked with sponge and orange cupped corals, and attracts a great deal of fish. There are almost always barracuda around the radar tower. Schools of permit are found here, too." The *Duane* and the *Bibb* have recently been upstaged by the *Spiegel Grove*, a 510-foot landing ship dock (for transporting the landing craft that carried combat troops to shore) that was sunk in 130 feet of water near Dixie Shoals. The *Spiegel Grove* (named somewhat inexplicably for the Ohio estate of President Rutherford B. Hayes, who left the office in 1881, some seventy years before the boat was commissioned) was sunk in 2002, after an arduous eight-year effort by the Key Largo Chamber of Commerce to have the ship brought down from its floating resting place on the James River in Virginia. When she was initially sent to the bottom, the *Spiegel Grove* came to rest on her starboard side. One of the few benefits of Hurricane Dennis's sweep across southern Florida in 2005 was that the storm righted the ship. "The size of the *Spiegel Grove* is intimidating," Stephen said. "You won't see it all in one dive, or even three. The first time people dive it, they're in sheer amazement at its size. Right now it's not as fishy as the *Duane*, perhaps because it's perpendicular to the current. That might change as it's down there longer. Still, it's the headliner now, and it delivers."

The positive attributes of Key Largo extend beyond its impressive wrecks. "The reefs are shallow and bright here," Stephen continued. "It's not overly intimidating diving. Much of the time, there's visibility of 60 feet; it's seldom worse than 30 feet. There's a great infrastructure, with professional operators and a variety of accommodations."

To help protect the reefs from the ravages of anchors, the Key Largo National Marine Sanctuary Program designed and installed mooring buoys at popular dive sites in the area. (The mooring buoys pioneered here are now used at many diving locales in the Caribbean and beyond.) Buoys mark the Key Largo Dry Rocks reef, where the bronze statue of Christ of

OPPOSITE
Fish life—here
French and Caesar
grunt—is quite
prolific around
Key Largo, thanks
to the protection
afforded by
early conservation
efforts.

13

DESTINATION

the Abyss rests, as well as the wreck of the *Benwood* and Molasses Reef. "I like a site on the south end of Molasses Reef called Fire Coral Caves," Stephen added. "There's always great pelagic activity, and resident Goliath groupers and Atlantic spadefish are also of interest."

STEPHEN FRINK is the world's most frequently published underwater photographer. He is the director of imaging technology for *Scuba Diving* magazine, and writes a monthly column on underwater photo trends and techniques. Stephen's work has also been published in a wide variety of general-interest publications such as *Natural History, Glamour, Time, Newsweek, Islands, Travel + Leisure, Esquire, Fortune, Forbes, Money,* as well as numerous National Geographic publications. He has also authored a coffee-table book entitled *Wonders of the Reef,* published by Harry N. Abrams. Stephen operates the Stephen Frink School of Underwater Photography in his home waters of Key Largo, Florida. Clients for assignment photography over the past twenty-four years have included Victoria's Secret, Mercury Marine, Henderson Aquatics, UK, Princeton Tec, Nikon, Canon, Aqualung, Scubapro, Jantzen, Mares, R.J. Reynolds, Seaquest, Oceanic, Club Med, and scores of resorts and live-aboard dive boats throughout the world. (See his work at www.stephenfrink.com.) Other Frink enterprises include a dive-travel company, WaterHouse Tours and Reservations (www.waterhousetours.com), specializing in exotic dive travel for underwater photographers and digital photo instruction. Stephen is also the exclusive North American and Caribbean distributor for the Austrian camera-housing manufacturer Seacam (www.seacamusa.com). He has invented and holds patents on a unique diver safety device (www.stephenfrink.com/sf-sos.php) consisting of a safety sausage utilizing a BC's pneumatics to inflate.

IF YOU GO

➤ **Getting There**: Key Largo is convenient to Miami, which is served by most carriers.

➤ **Best Time to Visit**: Diving is good year round at Key Largo, though summer months have the calmest conditions and best visibility.

➤ **Accommodations**: Key Largo/Florida Keys Tourism (800-822-1088; www.fla-keys.com/keylargo) lists a wide range of accommodations at this vacation hub.

➤ **Dive Shops/Guides**: Key Largo/Florida Keys Tourism lists many local dive shops.

DESTINATION 13

RANGIROA

RECOMMENDED BY **Paul Sloan**

Sometimes in the world of marketing and sales, one is presented with a daunting challenge—the old saw of the ice man hoping to sell his product to Eskimos comes to mind. In an earlier job, Paul Sloan was presented with a slightly less onerous task—selling French Polynesia as a diving destination.

"I had initially come down to French Polynesia to be a dive instructor," Paul began. "A few years later I returned to Los Angeles, and became director of marketing for French Polynesia Tourism. One of my personal mandates was to develop a niche for French Polynesia as a dive destination. The honeymooners that came to Tahiti and Moorea would certainly sometimes dive, but for ardent enthusiasts, French Polynesia wasn't quite on the map. Considering all that the region has to offer—big animals, warm water, clear water, easily accessible dive sites—it seemed a natural. And if I were going to focus on one French Polynesian island for its diving attributes, it would be Rangiroa."

French Polynesia encompasses 118 islands scattered across nearly one million square miles of the South Pacific Ocean, roughly 2,500 miles due south of the Hawaiian Islands. The islands—which vary from mountainous to nearly flat—are grouped under five archipelagos: Society, Marquesas, Tuamotu, Austral, and Gambier Islands. Tahiti is the most populated and best known island of Polynesia, immortalized in the paintings of Gauguin and generally celebrated as the prototypical tropical paradise (hence all those honeymooners); indeed, some refer to French Polynesia in its entirety as Tahiti. Rangiroa is part of the Tuamotu Archipelago, and is some 250 miles north of the island of Tahiti. It's considered the second-largest atoll in the world, made up of 240 small islets (or *motus* in local parlance) that form a 110-mile circle around a forty-two-mile-long/sixteen-mile-wide lagoon. Rangiroa translates as "huge sky" from the Polynesian language; the huge sky is the lagoon.

71

"Rangiroa offers three distinct diving experiences," Paul continued. "You can dive in the lagoon, on the drop-offs outside of the reef, or in the passes. The lagoon offers a very gentle diving experience—relatively shallow, clear water that's very calm. The name of one of the lagoon's better-known sites—The Aquarium—says it all. Outside the reef, along the walls, divers will see some of the big animals that Rangiroa is famous for—tuna, turtles, manta rays, Napoleon wrasse, sometimes bottlenose dolphins." Well-regarded ocean sites include Wrasse Plateau, The Big Blue, and The Wind Turbine.

If there's one experience that divers equate with Rangiroa, it's shooting the pass at Tiputa, considered by many as one of the diving world's great adrenaline rushes. Each day as high tide approaches, water rushes through the two passes (where the lagoon opens up to the sea), Tiputa and Avatoru, which are named for Rangiroa's two small towns. As the water charges in carrying baitfish and other goodies in its flow, larger animals take their places along the walls of the passage, looking for a meal . . . and divers follow to take in the show. Of the two passages, Tiputa is the most highly regarded. "A dive at Tiputa goes like this," Paul explained. "A boat drops you off outside the reef, a little bit above the pass and outside of the main current. You swim toward the current, and once it grabs you, the current brings you through. Forty minutes later, you pop up in the lagoon. At the peak of the tide, it's really moving—I'd say seven knots. When the *Tahiti Aggressor* dive boat was here, they established a PADI advanced certification for pass diving at Tiputa.

"Every time you go through the pass, you see different things. Some days it's a multitude of sharks, some days manta or spotted eagle rays, some days big schools of jacks and barracuda. You're just about guaranteed shark sightings on every dive—at least three or four, sometimes many more. The consistency of shark observations at Rangiroa has gained it a reputation as the 'shark-diving capital of the South Pacific.'" Sharks regularly observed at Rangiroa include gray reef, silvertip, silky, whitetip reef, blacktip reef, milk, sicklefin lemon, great hammerhead sharks, and, occasionally, tiger sharks.

"Toward the bottom of the pass there are caves," Paul added. "Sometimes you'll find sharks and other fish hanging out in these caves, other times you can pull in and get a foothold to watch the activity as it unfolds. When you're there gripping the bottom and you see dolphins and gray reef sharks swimming by, oblivious to the ripping current, you realize again how well suited they are to their environment."

By the way, it would seem that Paul was successful in his efforts. French Polynesia (and Rangiroa) is now regularly ranked among the world's top diving venues.

PAUL SLOAN learned to dive in the late 1970s while attending high school in the Monterey Bay, California area. He worked as a research diver for the University of California before becoming a scuba instructor in the late 1980s; he has managed diving schools in the Caribbean, in Mexico, and in the South Pacific. Paul formerly served as director of marketing for Tahiti Tourisme. He currently oversees the international marketing and distribution for the Gilbert Wane™ brand of Tahitian black eco-pearls environmentally grown in the pristine lagoon of Toau located within the Tuamotu UNESCO Biosphere Reserve. Paul holds a master's degree in tourism administration from the School of Business at the George Washington University, with specializations in marketing and sustainable tourism development, and a B.S. in environmental biology. He also holds professional certification in destination management from the International Institute for Tourism Studies (IITS), in conjunction with the World Tourism Organization (WTO) of the United Nations. Paul and his family currently reside in a marine protected area on the island of Moorea, French Polynesia, where he snorkels with his four-year-old son, Maui, every single chance he gets.

IF YOU GO

➤ **Getting There**: Rangiroa is reached via Papeete, Tahiti, on Air Tahiti (310-662-1860; http://airtahitinui-usa.com), which also provides flights from Los Angeles to Papeete.

➤ **Best Time to Visit**: Diving is excellent year round, though certain species are more prevalent in certain seasons.

➤ **Accommodations:** Hotel Kia Ora Resort features bungalows near Tiputa Pass. Tahiti Tourisme North America (877-Go-Tahiti; www.tahiti-tourisme.com) can outline other options.

➤ **Dive Shops/Guides**: There are six dive centers in Rangiroa, including Blue Dolphins (+68 99-60-301; www.bluedolphinsdiving.com) and Raie Manta Club (+68 99-68-480; http://raiemantaclub.free.fr/).

14

DESTINATION

ISLAND OF GRENADA

RECOMMENDED BY **Ethan Gordon**

Americans of a certain age may remember the tiny island nation of Grenada as the site of a short military invasion during the early Reagan years. Ethan Gordon thinks of Grenada as one of his favorite Caribbean diving venues. "You have a number of positive qualities at Grenada," Ethan began. "Topside, there's a lush, green island. The people of Grenada are extremely warm and outgoing. Below, you have something that's truly unique for the Caribbean, in fact for the world—the *Bianca C.*"

Grenada lies just south of the Windward Islands, with the Caribbean Sea to the south and west and the Atlantic to the east. The nation consists of the main island of Grenada (where most of the population resides) and eight smaller islands. Forged by volcanic activity, Grenada is mountainous, with one peak (Mount St. Catherine) reaching more than 2,700 feet. A rainforest thrives in the shadows of St. Catherine; much of the rest of the island is cloaked in a variety of spice plants—nutmeg, cinnamon, ginger, and cloves chief among them (Grenada is the world's second-largest producer of nutmeg, with Indonesia being the primary exporter). "When you get off the plane, you're struck by a terrific fragrance, the aroma of spices and flowers," Ethan said. "Between the mountains, the jagged coast, and the secret waterfalls you can hike into, Grenada is exactly what you'd envision a tropical island to be. There's a good infrastructure for visitors, in terms of hotels and other services. But all the hotels are locally owned; because there are no big flights that go in, there are no international chains. The character and charm of the island is intact."

And then there's the *Bianca C*—a 600-foot luxury cruise liner that rests upright at a depth of 165 feet near Whibble Reef, southwest of Grenada's capital city of St. George's. "The *Bianca C* is one of only a handful of luxury-liner wrecks in the world that can be reached by recreational divers," Ethan continued. "Some divers don't have the least bit of

OPPOSITE
The wreck of the
Bianca C *is the*
crown jewel of
Grenada diving.
Here, one of
the luxury liner's
davits—the device
used to lower down
the lifeboats—
is shown.

interest in wreck diving. To them, staring at a hunk of metal instead of a reef seems ridiculous. However, there's something special about the *Bianca C*. Even people who don't enjoy wrecks are drawn to it, and can dive it repeatedly."

The *Bianca C* began life in France as the *Maréchal Pétain*. Shortly after her launch in the spring of 1944, she was sunk near Port Bouc by retreating German naval forces. She was resurrected after the war and refitted as a cruise ship, *La Marseillaise*, and made her maiden voyage to Japan in 1949. After a brief stint as the *Arosa Sky* in 1957, she was sold to an Italian shipping firm in 1959 and rechristened the *Bianca C*. After further retrofitting, she began running a route from Naples to Venezuela, which included a stop in Grenada. During one of these stops off St. George's, on October 22, 1961, there was an explosion in the *Bianca C*'s boiler room, which led to a conflagration that's said to have brought the water around the ship to a boil. Thanks to the rapid response of the crew and the selfless assistance of St. George's residents, who swarmed to the ship in any vessel that would float to aid passengers, only two lives were lost. Soon the *Bianca C* was consumed by the sea a second—and final—time.

"Local dive shops like to call the *Bianca C* the 'Titanic of the Caribbean,'" Ethan said, "and in terms of sheer scale, the comparison is not overblown. When you're on the bottom at the front of the ship, the bow flares out at a height of six-and-a-half stories. The flared bow is reminiscent of the advertising posters the cruise lines used in the twenties and thirties. It's awe-inspiring." While the years are beginning to take their toll on the *Bianca C* (most of the central structure has imploded), much of its infrastructure remains intact, including the promenade decks and the foremast. Even one of the swimming pools on the deck is extant, allowing you to take a dip, as it were. One can't begin to take in the immensity of the *Bianca C* in one dive; at least two or three dives are necessary to make your way around the wreck.

A number of corals and sponges have taken up residence on the remnants of the *Bianca C*, in turn attracting an abundance of marine life, including Atlantic spadefish, moray eels, reef sharks, large barracudas, and rays. "I have to say that the *Bianca C* is perhaps my great photographic nemeses," Ethan confided. "Getting the shot I want, looking up at the flaring bow of the ship with a diver next to it for scale, has been hard to nail. The water can be a little murky at that depth, there's a little current, the sun goes in and out, and the threat of narcosis gives you very limited time at that depth. Every time I visit, I try to get this shot; the challenge keeps motivating me to go back. Hopefully I will get it soon. After almost fifty years at the bottom, the superstructure of the *Bianca C* is starting to cave in."

If the 100-plus-foot dive that a tour of the *Bianca C* entails is beyond your comfort level, Grenada offers a number of other wreck diving opportunities —twenty in total—in depths of as little as thirty feet. These include the freighter *HEMA 1* at ninety feet; the "Quarter Wreck" at thirty feet, which consists of the rear portions of a freight vessel; and the *San Juan*, a seventy-foot fishing vessel, also at ninety feet. "The *San Juan* rests on the Atlantic side of the island, in the middle of a barren plain," Ethan said. "Nurse sharks stack up around the boat like cord wood. I've seen them in there three or four sharks deep."

ETHAN GORDON is a freelance photojournalist focusing on diving, fishing, and travel. His work has taken him from the cold waters off New England to the Pacific Ocean, the Indian Ocean, the Coral Sea, and the Caribbean. Ethan has photographed thousands of marine creatures from around the world; his topside photography makes his assignment work stand out. Ethan has been honored twice by *Skin Diver* magazine and *Asian Diver*, which included his images in their prestigious Photo Annual Collector's Editions, and once by *Sport Diver*, which included one of his images in their first Photo Annual Collector's Edition. His work has been published in *National Geographic*, *Outside*, *Outdoor Life*, and many other magazines. From May 2005 to February 2008, Ethan served as editor of *Fathoms*. A PADI master scuba diver trainer, he has nearly 2,800 dives under his belt, and since 1989 has taught scuba diving to hundreds of people and has received awards for his teaching. Ethan holds a Bachelor of Architecture degree from Cornell University.

IF YOU GO

➤ **Getting There**: Grenada is served from the United States via Air Jamaica (800-523-5585; www.airjamaica.com) and American Airlines.
➤ **Best Time to Visit**: Winter and spring see less rain; June and November tend to be the wettest months during the rainy season.
➤ **Accommodations**: The Grenada Board of Tourism (473 440-2279; www.grenadagrenadines.com) highlights lodging options on the island of Grenada.
➤ **Dive Shops/Guides**: There are many dive shops serving Grenada; Ethan has had excellent experiences with Aquanauts Grenada (800-513-5257; www.aquanautsgrenada.com).

KONA

RECOMMENDED BY **Marty Snyderman**

Some would say that Hawaii is the Rodney Dangerfield of diving—it just doesn't get the respect it deserves. Marty Snyderman is in this camp. "For a long time, Hawaii had a reputation of lagging behind in the diving world. There was the perception that operators were more likely to take you to a place where they'd have the best chance to spear dinner, rather than show you the possibilities of the islands' marine life. I had a chance to dive out of Kona and other spots on Maui a fair amount six years ago, and was impressed with the quality of both the diving and the operators. When you talk to operators at some popular dive destinations and ask what's new, they'll talk about a new deal from an airline or the new chef in one of the restaurants. In Hawaii, they speak about new marine life they've come upon. The operators are genuinely excited, they love their marine animals. These guys live a diving lifestyle, they're ocean people. For me, that's fun to be around."

The eight islands that make up the Hawaiian archipelago comprise the most remote archipelago in the world; this last fact may often be forgotten, thanks to the ubiquity of pre-packaged vacations, which make the islands seem much closer than they are. The landmass of Hawaii boasts the world's largest proportion of endemic plant and animal species; it would be very rare indeed for nonnative bird species to find their way here, 2,500 miles from any continental landmass. The same is true for marine species. Scientists believe that more than 20 percent of Hawaii's fish, invertebrate, and coral populations are endemic; you simply won't see these animals anywhere else in the world. The island of Hawaii is the southeasternmost of the eight islands. The Kona coast is centrally situated on the island's west side.

"There's a saying that goes 'Hawaii has some of the ocean's most beautiful fishes, but no place to put them,'" Marty continued. "It's true that Hawaii doesn't have large reefs of brightly hued corals. The reefs were formed from lava, as were the islands. The steepness

OPPOSITE
If you wait long enough in the waters off Kona, something big—in this case, a humpback whale—will likely show up.

DESTINATION

16

of the islands carries right into the ocean, and the drop-offs are immense. In California, you might have to ride ten or twenty miles out to get to deep water. Off Kona (and many other places in Hawaii), you're in extremely deep water in ten minutes, with a good chance to see large pelagics. The open ocean bounding the islands is, in my opinion, the bluest, clearest water in the subtropics. When an open ocean animal presents itself, you see it very clearly. In some places, if you only have forty feet of visibility, you won't see that much of a forty-foot whale. Off Hawaii, you see that whale from a great distance, and watch it come into clearer and clearer view. You see the whole animal, the whole pod, and you see them well."

There are some eighty dive sites along the Kona coast, most within twenty minutes of shore. Many offer the chance to see big animals—spinner dolphins, silky sharks, tiger sharks, hammerheads, humpback whales, and sometimes even sperm whales. One of the seminal diving experiences around Kona is the nocturnal manta ray dive, reputed as the most reliable manta sighting dive in the world. "The night-time manta ray feed is a surreal experience," Marty continued. "All the dive shop operators go to the same spot. Divers are given lights to shine up from the bottom to attract plankton. When the plankton arrive, the manta rays generally come in. We've had as many as seventeen at one time—the record is something like twenty-eight or twenty-nine at one time. As they are feeding, the rays do these graceful backflips, inches away from you. Though I prefer to see these animals under natural conditions, the manta dive is a magical experience."

"My experiences in Hawaii allowed me to see aspects of ocean life that I hadn't seen in thirty years of diving," Marty said. "The open-water dives are particularly compelling. You're in sight of land, but when you step off the boat, you're going into thousands of feet of water. They have buoys on chains out there, and you swim down and hang off one of these chains that stretch thousands of feet, hoping that some Godzilla will come by. You feel like a piece of bait. You feel vulnerable, little, naked. It's an adrenaline pumper. You know everything will be okay, but I still get butterflies when I do it. It's just you, staring into the blue, with an incredible sense of anticipation; it makes me think of how keyed up you'd be before being in a major sporting event. Then Godzilla shows up—an oceanic white-tip shark or a pod of pilot whales—and everything's cool. Everything out there swims so much better than you. It's humbling, but it's also a privilege. There have been other dives in the winter when I can listen to the songs of humpbacks for the entire time I'm underwater. I may not see them, but I hear them. There's something about that that helps me put in perspective that it's a big ocean and a big planet and we're just part of it.

"I truly believe that if the world's politicians and policy makers had such experiences, the environment wouldn't be on the fiftieth back burner."

MARTY SNYDERMAN is a still photographer, film producer, author, and speaker specializing in the marine environment. He is the marine-life editor for *Dive Training* magazine, where his work is featured monthly. Marty's photography and/or writing has also been featured in *National Geographic* magazine, numerous National Wildlife Federation publications, *Natural History*, *Time*, and *Newsweek*, and has been used by the Monterey Bay Aquarium, New England Aquarium, Sea World, Seattle Aquarium, and numerous other publications and organizations. He has authored nine books, including *California Marine Life*, which has just been revised and rereleased in cooperation with the Monterey Bay Aquarium, and *Guide to Marine Life of the Caribbean, Bahamas, and Florida*. An Emmy Award–winning cinematographer, his film *The Secret World of Sharks and Rays* premiered during October of 1998 on the PBS series *Nature*. Marty produced and filmed *To Be with Sharks (View from the Cage)*, the second most widely watched premiere in the history of Discovery Channel's Shark Week. In addition, his cinematography was featured in Warner Bros.' *Free Willy* and in features from the National Geographic Society, *Nova*, the British Broadcasting Corporation, and many other broadcast outlets. Marty has an online photo course where students can work through the different courses at their own pace; visit www.martysnyderman.com for more details.

IF YOU GO

➤ **Getting There**: Kona, on the island of Hawaii, has direct service from Los Angeles on American and United Airlines, and is served via Honolulu by a number of carriers.
➤ **Best Time to Visit**: You can dive Kona year round with little variation in conditions; humpbacks are present November to May.
➤ **Accommodations**: A comprehensive list of lodgings options is available from the Big Island Visitors Bureau (808-961-5797; www.bigisland.org).
➤ **Dive Shops/Guides**: There are a number of dive shops serving the Kona coast, including KonaHonu Divers (888-333-4668; www.konahonudivers.com).

UTILA

RECOMMENDED BY **Adam Laverty**

Modern life in the affluent Western world is sometimes characterized as a quest for balance. Satisfying work, but not too much of it; quality time with the family, but some "alone time," too. Many extend the balancing act to their leisure time. Good diving is important, but so is an interesting onshore experience.

For Adam Laverty, the Honduran island of Utila strikes a perfect balance. "I used to work in Egypt and Thailand," Adam began. "In Egypt, the diving was amazing, but the atmosphere on land was less so. I found the people and the food and the general ambiance in Thailand beautiful, but the diving in the Gulf wasn't quite first rate. Utila offers both fine diving and an extremely comfortable land environment. It's very laid back, no hurry hurry, rush rush. The people who live and work on the island go out of their way to make everyone feel welcome. Within two or three days, people are calling you by your first name. I came here initially to do my Instructor exams, and planned to stay a year. I'm now in my fifth year."

The smallest of the three major Bay Islands (which include better-known Roatan), Utila lies roughly eighteen miles north of the mainland port city of La Ceiba in the western Caribbean. Just twelve square miles in size, Utila has a population that hovers around 2,500 residents, most in and around the town of East Harbor (sometimes simply referred to as Utila). There are more than sixty dive sites around Utila, varying from wrecks and caves to wall dives. (The Mesoamerican Barrier Reef reaches its southern terminus near the Bay Islands, with depths plunging to more than 3,000 feet east of the reef.) Historically, Utila has had a following among the backpacker set as one of the Caribbean's most value-oriented diving destinations. Bargain hunters can still find extremely reasonable packages on the island, though resorts offering more luxurious amenities have opened their doors in the last few years. "You have quite a range," Adam continued, "from dorm rooms for three dollars to five dollars a night to a high-end place like Deep Blue Resort that's more than $1,500 a week.

"Utila has many different reef systems, with habitats ranging from shallow, sandy sites to sheer drop-offs. Conditions are great year round for divers of all levels; it's generally very calm, with very little in the way of currents. As for favorite spots, I have a number of them. The Duppy Waters—'duppy' means ghost in local slang—is a steep wall dive in Turtle Harbor. When you swim over the edge, it seems to open up forever. You have horse-eye jack, Creole wrasse, great barracuda, giant barrel sponges, and hammerheads cruising by. Blackish Point, also on the north side of the island, is a perfect drift drive dive site with a gentle current and caverns. At Black Hills, a sea mount off the east side of the island, you're guaranteed to come upon large aggregations of Atlantic spadefish, as well as resident turtles. A year ago, I was at a site called Black Coral Wall. We came over a sandy patch, and a Hawksbill turtle came up, looked each diver in the eye, swam around us in a circle, and actually tried to recline on one diver's hand. If you're here in the spring or fall, you're almost sure to see whale sharks. I've had dives where I had a thirty-footer in front of the boat, a twenty-foot specimen off the back, and a pair of dolphins in the middle. I had to ask myself, 'Where do I look first?'"

It is the gargantuan whale shark that many divers travel to Utila to experience. Whale sharks are the world's largest fish; the largest specimen ever officially recorded was more than forty-one feet in length, though stories of fifty- and even sixty-foot species abound. (The average length of the whale sharks around Utila is between twenty and thirty feet, weight between fifteen and twenty tons; larger specimens are believed to achieve a lifespan of over one hundred years.) Despite their tremendous size, these creatures are quite placid, subsisting on plankton. They feed by opening their mouths and trapping the microorganisms. After closing its mouth, the shark uses gill rakers, thousands of bristly structures about 10 cm long, to clean the captured prey from its gills. Anything that doesn't pass through the gills is consumed. Whale sharks are solitary travelers, and are generally found in deep waters of the open ocean. No one completely understands what brings so many whale sharks to the waters around Utila, though some researchers think that the waters on the north part of the island may be on the animals' migratory path. In a study conducted by Scott Eckert and Brent Stewart of Deep Blue Utila in conjunction with Hubbs Sea World Research Institute, one animal tagged off Utila was shown to travel upward of 8,000 miles in the course of three years. Scientists hope to gain a greater understanding of whale shark behavior through the efforts of the Utila Whale Shark Research Project.

"Whale sharks and other large pelagics are exciting and awe inspiring," Adam ventured, "but as we don't get to see these amazing animals every day, I find that the personality of little fish goes a long way. For me, frogfish have tons of personality, as do spiny-head blenny. One of my favorites around Utila is the yellow-headed jawfish. They're only about two inches long, and they use their mouths to burrow into the sand. When it's mating time, the male comes out of the burrow and does a little dance to lure a mate. He flares his lips and prances about with his fins by his side, like a little Mick Jagger on the stage. After he takes her into his den and does his procreative business, he carries the eggs in his mouth to guard them."

ADAM LAVERTY is a diving instructor at Alton's Dive Center (www.altonsdiveshop.com) on Utila and specializes in Underwater Photography, whale sharks, and all marine life in general. Adam learned to dive on the island of Kho Tao in the gulf of Thailand while on vacation and fell in love with it straight away. He has dived throughout South East Asia, Egypt, England, and Central America, working as a Dive Master in both Thailand and Egypt. For the last 5 years he has instructed and guided divers around the beautiful reefs of Utila. Before fulltime diving, Adam worked in the hedge fund industry and studied European History at the University of East Anglia.

IF YOU GO

➤ **Getting There**: Most visitors will reach Utila via Roatan, which is served by American, Continental, and TACA (1-800-400-TACA; www.taca.com). From Roatan, it's a quick shuttle flight to Utila on Aerolineas Sosa (+50 44-25-3166) or Atlantic Airlines International (+50 44-25-3364; www.atlanticairlinesint.com).

➤ **Best Time to Visit**: Utila dives well the year round, but if you're interested in encountering whale sharks, your best bet is March through May and August through October.

➤ **Accommodations**: AboutUtila.com lists the broad range of lodging options available at Utila.

➤ **Dive Shops/Guides**: There are many dive shops in Utila, including Captain Morgan's (225-341-4564; www.divingutila.com). View a complete list at AboutUtila.com.

DESTINATION 17

KOMODO NATIONAL PARK

RECOMMENDED BY **Greg Heighes**

If one were to pen an advertising slogan for Komodo National Park, it might go something like this: "Come for the dragons. Stay for the diving."

"In 1988, I took some time off from university to work as a dive guide on a live-aboard that cruised about Indonesia," Greg Heighes began. "I dove throughout the region, including Komodo National Park. I didn't have much experience then, and one diving spot seemed much like the next. The more I heard the feedback from guests, however, the more I realized how special Komodo National Park is. As we sailed around Indonesia, the boat's captain would set aside more time on the boat's itinerary for Komodo. There's something here for all dive personalities—recreational divers, photographers, and thrill seekers."

The region of Komodo encompasses a string of volcanic islands in eastern Indonesia, resting between the larger landmasses of Sumbawa and Flores, roughly 230 miles east of Bali. Most of the area is contained in Komodo National Park, a 700-square-mile protected area that includes the larger islands of Komodo, Rinca, Gili Mota, Nusa Kode, and Padar. The park was established in 1980, largely to protect dwindling populations of the world's largest lizards; it was listed as a UNESCO World Heritage site in recognition of its unique animal life above and below the surface of the surrounding Flores Sea. Like the Lombok Strait to the west, the Komodo region serves as a funnel between the Indian and Pacific Oceans. The flow of water and accompanying nutrients make for a rich stew that sustains robust sea life, including over 250 species of coral, 1,000 species of fish, and marine mammals ranging from passing blue whales to dugongs, members of the manatee family that live solely in salt water.

"There's a tremendous range of dive environments in Komodo National Park," Greg continued, "ranging from pinnacles and walls to sea mounts and passages, with about

everything in between. I've heard the area described as an inverse of Bali. There, the terrestrial vegetation is very rich and lush, but the marine environment a bit less interesting. Around Komodo, the islands are very dry, but the marine life is incredibly prolific and diverse. Others have called Komodo the Galápagos of the Asia Pacific. This is not inaccurate, as you do see a meeting of Asian and Australian species on the island of Flores (which lies near the Wallace Line), and you do have the exchange of Indian and Pacific Ocean species. Then again, such observers may be linking the two places together by the fact that both sets of islands have great diving and distinctive reptilian life."

Many Komodo dive sites are subject to strong currents, but divers with local knowledge can work this to their advantage. "There's a spot called Castle Rock," Greg said. "We'll drop in about a hundred yards or so above the rocks, which are submerged fifteen feet or so, swim down, and then drift through with the current. As you drift, you'll see massive schools of smaller fish, all the planktonic feeders. Suddenly, the baitfish will start fleeing in every direction as dogtooth tuna and trevally dart in at incredible speeds for a meal; they're moving so quickly, they're just a flash." Another of Greg's favorite spots is Batu Bolong, a small rock island between Komodo and Tatawa island. "There's life on every inch of this pinnacle," Greg continued, "it's as if marine creatures were fighting for a place to attach themselves." Coral and invertebrates are the stars toward the top of Batu Bolong; farther down, you'll often be greeted by Napoleon wrasse, giant trevally, and large schools of rainbow runners, with mantas sometimes flapping through.

Komodo is not all about sweeping currents and bigger fish. "In the south of the park there are sites with stunningly beautiful invertebrate life, the kind of creatures that make photographers go gaga," Greg said. "Though I dive around Komodo quite regularly, I'm always coming upon things I haven't seen before, which is always a delight." Perhaps the most notable southern site is Cannibal Rock. Decorated in soft corals (including immense purple gorgonian fans), vibrant sea apples, and sea cucumbers, this sea mount is macro heaven, with a host of wildly hued nudibranchs, Coleman shrimp, pygmy sea horses, and frogfish.

No visitors to the Komodo Islands will want to leave before meeting the region's most famous inhabitant, the Komodo dragon. The largest member of the monitor lizard family—and the world's largest lizard—Komodo dragons average nearly eight feet in length and weigh between 120 and 150 pounds; the largest recorded specimen reached nearly ten

OPPOSITE
Imperial shrimp
are among the
fascinating
macro life you'll
find at spots like
Cannibal Rock.

18

DESTINATION

feet in length and 366 pounds. The dragons feed primarily on the island's small Timor deer, but have been known to eat eggs (of other dragons and turtles), buffalo, boar, wild horses, and monkeys. Though fairly agile, they rely on the element of surprise to overcome prey. Though Komodo dragons will sometimes be seen near the water, reclining on beaches or rocky ledges, a walking tour with officials of the Komodo National Park can virtually guarantee an encounter, especially near the ranger stations, as the smell of food draws them in. Dragon numbers have been impacted by declining populations of deer, though the current population is holding steady at roughly 3,000.

"I've had the experience of watching dragons take down a deer in the wild," Greg recalled. "One animal had his jaw latched onto the leg of the deer, and was starting to drag it back toward the brush. Its tail was really thrashing, clearing brush as he moved backward. Another dragon appeared from the woods and grabbed another leg of the deer in its jaws. The sound of their thrashing and growling was chilling. On another occasion, I did a four-hour hike on the island of Rinca with a ranger I know. We were up in the hills, in long grass, when the ranger pointed out two large dragons, walking with a pincer movement, like army soldiers. They were clearly at the top of the food chain, and clearly hunting. You really sensed their presence, that they knew who was boss."

GREG HEIGHES is a divemaster and has been leading live-aboard dive trips with a focus on Komodo National Park since 2000. He learned to dive alongside his famous aunt and uncle, Valerie and Ron Taylor. Greg operates Dive Komodo with his brother Mark Heighes.

IF YOU GO

➤ **Getting There:** Labuhanbajo on the island of Flores is a common departure point for live-aboards. To reach Labuhanbajo, you'll fly to Densapar, Bali, which is served from Los Angeles by a number of carriers, including China Airlines and Cathay Pacific. From Densapar, flights to Labuhanbajo are offered on GT Air and Trans Nusa; scheduled flights fluctuate somewhat, and dive operators recommend you book flights with their assistance to insure that connections are made.

DESTINATION 18

➤ **Best Time to Visit**: Live-aboards ply Komodo National Park the year round. Komodo is very dry most of the year, though it does experience a monsoon season in January and February.

➤ **Accommodations**: Several live-aboards operate in Komodo National Park, including Dive Komodo (+62 385-41862; www.divekomodo.com), which runs retrofitted *phinisis*, the traditional sailing craft of Indonesia.

18

DESTINATION

LEMBEH STRAITS

RECOMMENDED BY **Chuck Nicklin**

Say "Lembeh Straits" in muck diving circles, and eyes are sure to sparkle. After all, this is the epicenter of critter diving. Chuck Nicklin put it plainly: "No place I've ever been gives you the opportunity to photograph more exotic animals in such easy diving conditions as Lembeh Straits."

Lembeh Straits is a narrow body of water running along the eastern edge of the province of North Sulawesi, Indonesia, where an arm of the Sulawesan landmass stretches out between the Celebes and Molucca seas. Just ten miles long and a little more than a mile wide, the straits take their name from Lembeh Island, which lies in these waters to the east. From the boat, Lembeh Straits is not exactly inviting. It lacks the clarity that many might associate with these temperate waters; some have even called it dirty. Even the bottom itself has little variation beyond its black sand and an occasional strand of coral. But it's in the sand—the muck, as it were—that the magic happens for those who "go slow and look down." What seems like a lifeless blank becomes, under closer scrutiny, a teeming ecosystem.

Muck diving is a relatively recent phenomenon, the practice (and moniker) popularized by Bob Halstead during night dives from the famed craft the *Telita* in Milne Bay, Papua New Guinea, in the 1980s. On such sandy (or otherwise soft) bottoms, divers search for the smaller, often fascinating creatures that dwell in the sediment, creatures that had largely been ignored before advances in underwater macrophotography made it possible to capture these "critters" in all of their glory. Divers began discovering Lembeh in the early nineties. "I had some friends who came back from North Sulawesi with some great macro shots, which piqued my interest," Chuck recalled. "I had other friends that operated a boat called *Aqua One* in Thailand, and they started going south to Sulawesi and Lembeh Straits. I arranged a trip with them, and after a few dives, started getting excited. I had a chance to shoot with

OPPOSITE

Many of the creatures of Lembeh Straits have yet to be formally classified — including this unidentified species of octopus.

DESTINATION

19

high-definition cameras, which yielded some wonderful shots (some of the photos were later shown at DENA). I've been down many times since."

"Mesmerizing." "Astounding." "Exhilarating." These are the adjectives that visitors most frequently apply to the diminutive denizens of Lembeh Straits. The sea horse family is well represented, with several species of pygmies, as well as mandarinfish, ghost pipefish, and the stunning endemic Banggai cardinalfish. You'll also find Ambon scorpionfish, devil fish, fingered dragonets, wonderpus, stonefish, mimic octopus, frogfish, harlequin shrimp, candy crabs, bobtail squid, and snake eels, not to mention a seemingly limitless array of nudibranchs. For Chuck, cuttlefish are a great Lembeh attraction. "On a recent trip, I was able to photograph some hatching cuttlefish. They were only about an inch long, even more colorful than the adults I encountered. As they hatched, there were tiny crabs trying to eat them. Capturing this on film was very special to me."

An appealing aspect of the Lembeh experience is the simplicity of the program. "There's no question that it's a long journey to get to North Sulawesi," Chuck continued, "but once you're there, it's quite easy. Diving is right in front of your lodge—five or ten minutes in the boat, a half hour at most, and you're ready to go in the water. It's very relaxed. You can go out, make a dive, come back, have a snack and reload your film, go out for another dive, have lunch, do another dive, take a nap, then go out for a night dive. Three or four dives a day is commonplace."

There are more than thirty dive sites commonly visited in the Lembeh Straits, enough to satisfy the growing number of macro fanatics. Most sites are in relatively shallow water—forty to fifty feet—and currents are light. A few better-known venues include Hair Ball (a haven for frogfish) and Police Pier (a favorite night-diving spot, where scorpionfish and lionfish lie in wait). Though most make the long trek to Lembeh for the muck, some reef diving and even one wreck are available. Within a few hours are other sites that highlight North Sulawesi's tremendous species variety (more than 3,000 species are found here). Whether in the muck or on adjoining reefs, most divers will find themselves fumbling for their fish ID books to figure out what they've seen.

"It's my guess that this part of the world will see more and more divers, as its popularity grows," Chuck added. "The resorts and their divemasters are aware that dive opportunities will become depreciated if they don't properly take care of their animals. After all, you can only have a camera housing bang up against sea fan so many times before that sea fan is no more."

CHARLES "CHUCK" NICKLIN was in the retail diving business as the owner of San Diego's Diving Locker for forty-two years. A career underwater cinematographer, he has traveled the world filming Hollywood features and documentaries. Now retired from retail, Chuck and his wife, Roz (an accomplished still photographer), lead diving trips around the world through Chuck Nicklin Travel (www.chucknicklin.com).

IF YOU GO

➤ **Getting There**: From the U.S., travelers will generally fly to Singapore on Singapore Airlines (800-742 3333; www.singaporeair.com), then on to Manado, Indonesia.
➤ **Best Time to Visit**: Diving at Lembeh is consistent year round.
➤ **Accommodations**: A number of dive resorts serve Lembeh. Chuck generally stays at Kasawari Resort (+62 811-436-222; www.kasawari-lembeh.com).

19

DESTINATION

NUSA LEMBONGAN

RECOMMENDED BY **Roger Munns**

Oceanic sunfish—or mola mola—are occasionally seen by sailors or fishermen as they "sunbathe" at the surface. Often times, their dorsal fins are mistaken for those of sharks. While surface sightings are not infrequent, opportunities to dive with them are quite rare. For several months each year off a small island southeast of Bali, mola mola congregate in considerable numbers, allowing divers an excellent chance to interact with these reclusive creatures. "The mola mola come very regularly to a site called the Blue Corner at Nusa Lembongan," Roger Munns explanied. "You're almost guaranteed to see one there. Oddly enough, I used to go to Bali for surfing, and one of the great breaks was at a place called Shipwrecks. Shipwrecks is only fifty or one hundred yards away from the Blue Corner—though until recently, the sunfishes' visits to Blue Corner were not well documented."

Bali is the best known of the islands of Indonesia, thanks to its popularity as a tourist destination. Its steep volcanic mountains and pristine white-and-black-sand beaches are the picture of tropical bliss. Nusa Lembongan is twelve miles from Bali, resting in the midst of the Lombok Strait, along with its neighbors, Nusa Penida and Nusa Ceningan. This strait is part of the Indonesian Throughflow, a key point for water exchange between the Indian and Pacific Oceans. (The section of the Lombok Strait between Bali and Lembongan is called the Badung Strait.) Lembongan is also situated almost directly along the Wallace Line (named for British naturalist Sir Alfred Wallace), which designates the biological division between Asia and Australia/Oceania. Being in the path of the Indonesian Throughflow, the currents around Lembongan can be extremely strong; it's not terrain for beginners. Thanks to the currents, which funnel cold water upwellings from a deep trench north of Nusa Penida, water temperatures can vary wildly, by as much as ten to fifteen degrees. "The thermaclines

OPPOSITE
Nusa Lembongan is one of the few places in the world where mola mola can be seen underwater with regularity.

DESTINATION 20

are incredible," Roger continued. "You can extend your hand and the water can be eight or ten degrees cooler. It's quite mad! The great currents also carry tremendous quantities of macrobiotic life past Lembongan, which nurtures coral and fish life and starts a chain of feeding."

The waters around Lembongan boast healthy reefs and even opportunities to observe fine macro life, and the island's proximity to strong flows and deep water make it a regular stomping ground for pelagics—manta and eagle rays, white-tip and black-tip shark, tuna, and giant trevally among them. But it's the excellent odds of swimming with mola mola that draws many divers to Lembongan. The word "mola" is Latin for millstone, and the added emphasis of *two* millstones speaks to the density of the strange creatures. (Their German name—*Schwimmender kopf*—translates as "swimming head," and that says a lot!) Nearly as tall as they are long, mola mola average a ton and change in weight, with some specimens growing as large as several tons, with a height (including fins) of more than ten feet. Lacking proper tails, they propel their girth along by moving their dorsal and anal fins in a sculling motion. To maintain their weight, mola mola consume vast amounts of jellyfish; they are in turn preyed upon by orcas, sea lions, and larger sharks. Research suggests they spend most of their time at depths of over 600 feet, though relatively little is known about their habits. The fish seem averse to cooler water temperatures (in the low fifties); some believe their basking behavior could be a means of warming up.

There are several spots around Lembongan where mola mola are regularly found in the summer months, but Blue Corner is the most reliable—and best known (it's variously known as Jurassic or Ental Point). "There's a sloping reef at the top section, with a proliferation of soft and hard coral," Roger explained. "You follow the current around a corner, and then there's a vertical wall that drops to one hundred feet and more. This is the spot where you see the mola mola." The sunfish come into the relative shallows against the reef to be cleaned of parasites by schools of bannerfish who comb them of the small critters that call them home. "They'll rise and settle anywhere between thirty and 130 feet, and point their nose toward the surface at a forty-five-degree angle," Roger continued, "and the bannerfish will rise to meet them. Considering the size of the mola mola and the number of parasites they carry, it's a huge feed; butterfly fish also come in for a bite. While they're being cleaned, the mola mola are very approachable, even placid. But when they're coming into cleaning stations, they're very skittish. Sometimes divers will rush out to meet them, and they're out of there like a bat out of hell. The bottom line is, be patient and wait for the cleaning process to begin before you approach." The best conditions for encountering mola mola are when there's enough tidal flow to draw them in, but not so much as to spoil visibility.

"My best interaction with a mola mola came while filming a segment of *Great Ocean Adventures with Monty Halls*," Roger added. "Fellow Scubazooer Simon Christopher was filming Monty; I was taking photographs. We had one animal that was oblivious to us, at about one hundred feet down. We swam around with him for almost thirty minutes. He swam about the reef a bit, then would stop for a clean. We'd switch off; I'd shoot, then Simon would shoot. It was really bizarre to have that kind of opportunity. That one dive I had more time with a mola mola than all the other days put together."

ROGER MUNNS is a senior cameraman with Scubazoo (www.scubazoo.com). Before joining Scubazoo, he traveled extensively, surfing and snowboarding; it was during a flat surf spell in Byron Bay that Roger took the opportunity to learn to dive. Since then, diving has been his main passion. Roger has been involved in a number of Scubazoo's broadcast productions, including projects for the BBC's natural history unit, the World Wildlife Fund, Dorling Kindersley, and Four Seasons hotels and resorts. Roger is also an accomplished underwater photographer; his photos and articles have appeared in many publications around the world, as well as in Scubazoo's first coffee table book, *Sipadan, Mabul, and Kapalai—Sabah's Underwater Treasure*. He particularly enjoys the color and abstract shapes that can be found in macrophotography. Roger studied mathematics at Nottingham University.

![IF YOU GO]

➤ **Getting There**: First you'll need to get to Densapar, Bali, which is served from Los Angeles by China Airlines and Cathay Pacific. From Densapar, you'll need to take a boat to Lembongan; your hotel can generally arrange boat service.

➤ **Best Time to Visit**: The rainy season is from December to February; the weather is very consistent the remainder of the year. Mola mola are present July through October.

➤ **Accommodations**: World Diving Lembongan lists a range of lodging options on their Website (www.world-diving.com).

➤ **Dive Shops/Guides**: There are several dive operators on Lembongan, including World Diving Lembongan (+62 81-239-00686; www.world-diving.com).

RAJA AMPAT

RECOMMENDED BY **Berkley White**

Five hundred sixty-five species of hard coral (and counting). One thousand one hundred species of reef fish (and counting). Six hundred species of mollusks (and counting). Experts ranging from the Nature Conservancy to ichthyologist Dr. Gerald Allen (who counted 283 fish species on ONE dive!) to coral specialist Dr. John Veron agree—Raja Ampat may very well have the richest coral reefs and fish diversity of any place in the world. "The density of the soft-coral reefs around there is simply staggering," began Berkley White. "Divers who were drawn to Fiji and Palau for their coral and fish diversity will be overwhelmed by Raja Ampat. It embodies a wild, virgin ecosystem; it's the Amazon rainforest of under-water diversity."

Raja Ampat (or Four Kings) is an archipelago of 1,500 small islands and shoals off the northwest tip of the Bird's Head Peninsula on the Indonesian province of West Papua (formerly known as Irian Jaya). There are four larger islands in the archipelago—Waigeo, Salawati, Batanta, and Misool; in total, the area comprises some 15,000 square miles of land and sea, and rests in the heart of the coral triangle formed by the reefs of northern Australia, Indonesia, the Philippines, and New Guinea. It's here that currents from the surround-ing regions meet, creating an especially rich environment for sustaining life. "The waters around Raja Ampat are emerald blue when the visibility is at its highest," Berkley continued. "There are times when the nutrients are so thick, the water can go completely green, to the point where impeded visibility can impact the diving. While I have colleagues who have experienced poor conditions, I've spent three months over the last three years there, and have always enjoyed good visibility."

Raja Ampat also benefits from low human impact; there are relatively few residents in the immediate area, and a vast majority of those are subsistence fishermen. That being

OPPOSITE
A snorkeler
explores a cave
near Misool
Island in the
waters of Raja
Ampat.

said, there is evidence of dynamite fishing (attributed to Thai and Filipino commercial fishing entities) and concern that illegal logging on some islands will bring siltation to the reefs, killing coral. Conservation advocates are pushing to have Raja Ampat named a UNESCO World Heritage site. If this occurs, current conservation measures will gain more teeth.

When diving around Raja Ampat, one has the sense of pioneering new marine terrain—largely because you are! "There's one operator from the Netherlands—Max Ammer—who's been diving here for almost fifteen years," Berkley explained. "He identified many of the current sites. The first dive boats appeared in 2002, but Raja Ampat has only really caught the eye of the diving world in the last three years. I imagine people will be finding new sites for fifty years to come, though it's hard to get motivated to do much exploring, as the existing sites are so tremendous. There are pinnacles with dense, soft-coral reef systems and excellent densities of fish; fifteen minutes away, there are mangrove systems with soft coral growing right up to the water's edge, on the roots of the mangroves. These areas are a crazy mix of jungle meets ocean habitat, a rainbow of colors with brackish-water fish, like archerfish, that you'd expect to find in the Amazon. There are even fjordlike spots filled with jellyfish that move from one side of the water to the other with the sun. There are sea fans bigger than humans, and almost every site we dove had an immense number of pygmy sea horses. Whatever you're after—critters, color, reef fish—Raja Ampat is diving on a grand scale."

Nearly every dive around Raja Ampat holds wonders and surprises, but two sites especially stand out for Berkley. The first is the limestone cliffs of the islet of Farondi, east of Misool. "It's soft-coral mania," Berkley enthused. "One of the most amazing gardens on the planet, and great critters, too. Another site that gets people pumping is the Passage (sometimes called Kabui Passage), a narrow channel that runs between Waigeo and Gam islands. This is one place where you get the transition from reef to mangrove. It feels like a jungle river, and when the tide is at full bore, it can be a roller-coaster ride—though there are plenty of places where you can 'eddy out' of the current. You can dive it whatever the tide; when you've had enough and the current is running, you can ride the tide with the bumphead parrotfish that patrol the channel.

"There are many times when diving enthusiasts travel to the other side of the planet, and have far more intimate encounters with animals than with people," Berkley reflected. "Part of that comes from the isolation of being on a dive boat. Still, it's nice to have contact with the people of the place you're visiting." Berkley shared two such interactions he experienced in Raja Ampat—one planned, one much less so. "A few other divers and I had ridden the Passage on the inbound tide. The other divers decided to head back out; I hung back so I could ride the tide out. As I floated along in the current, I popped out periodically to make sure I hadn't drifted too far. I popped up in one eddy, and there was a dugout canoe against the shore. 'Wow!' I thought. 'Someone made their way in while I was under.' There was a little cave next to where the canoe was pulled out, and there was a Papuan man in the cave—curly hair, dark skin, very distinctive from other Indonesians. He had a spear in his hand, and he wore a loinclothlike garment. He was looking at me with all my techie gear as though I'd just dropped out of space. We stared at each other for what must have been five minutes. Eventually, he backed into the cave and I dropped underwater and moved on. I have to think that he still thinks about the strange being he saw in the Passage; I certainly think about him.

"If our schedule permits, I love to bring guests into the small villages on the islands. Some guests want to deliver toys and school supplies to the children. We're always well received. On some occasions, the villagers will come out to the boat; to them, we must appear as the craziest-looking things on the planet. Part of our daily routine is to share the day's best photos on a screen with everyone on the boat. If we're near a village, we may put up one of the boat's sails and project the pictures there. Villagers will sometimes come out in their dugouts—eighty or one hundred people—to watch the slide show. As each critter comes up on the sail, we hear the villagers 'ooh' and 'ahh.'"

BERKLEY WHITE is a leading expert in the field of underwater photography and digital image processing. As a professional photographer and instructor, he shares his in-field photographic techniques and digital methods through a series of select travel events each year. Berkley is the founder of Backscatter (www.backscatter.com) in Monterey, California, the largest specialty underwater photographic supplier in the US, and is the organizer of international photographic events such as the Digital Shootout.

IF YOU GO

➤ **Getting There**: Sorong, West Papua, is the staging point for many Raja Ampat expeditions. From the U.S., travelers will generally fly to Singapore on Singapore Airlines (800-742-3333; www.singaporeair.com), then on to Manado, Indonesia. After a night's stay in Manado, you travel on to Sorong.

➤ **Best Time to Visit**: October and November have low winds and the lightest rainfall, though one can dive Raja Ampat year round.

➤ **Accommodations**: Many traveling to Raja Ampat will favor a live-aboard to cover the most ground. A number of companies serve the region; Berkley has had good experiences with Kararu Dive Voyages (+62 361-282-931; http://kararu.com). Papua Diving (+62 951-328-038; www.papua-diving.com), which pioneered underwater adventures in Raja Ampat, offers several on-shore lodging options on the island of Kri.

DESTINATION 21

WAKATOBI NATIONAL PARK

RECOMMENDED BY **Ken Knezick**

Ken Knezick has strong feelings about Wakatobi National Park: "Wakatobi has presented me with the most beautiful, healthy, diverse, and pristine reefs I've ever had the pleasure of diving," he began. "And I have to say that Wakatobi Dive Resort is one of the most remarkable dive-oriented operations I've ever visited." Considering that Ken is a dive-travel expert with twenty-five years experience and more than 3,000 dives to his credit, that's saying something.

The three-and-a-half-million-acre Wakatobi National Park lies off the southeastern tip of the Indonesian province of Sulawesi, in the Banda Sea. Its name is an anagram of the first two letters of the four main islands in the region—Wangi-Wangi, Kaledupa, Tomia, and Binongko, the islands of Wakatobi, combined with the area's many other smaller islands, are referred to as the Tukang Besi Archipelago. Wakatobi is considered one of the most biologically diverse areas in the world, with more coral genera than any place else on the planet. As such, the region has been a focal point for conservation and sustainable fishery efforts championed by the Nature Conservancy, the World Wildlife Fund, and Operation Wallacea.

"There are three reasons that I find myself going back to Wakatobi," Ken continued. "The ease of the diving, the beauty and pristine quality of the reef, and the frequency and quality of wildlife encounters. Wakatobi is not the best place to come upon big pelagics, though you'll sometimes see them, too. On one occasion, I had a baby whale shark swim within five feet of me as I hovered on the surface after a dive; it was like a gift from Baruna, the Indonesian god of the sea. But for tropical fish and invertebrates, Wakatobi is hard to beat. I think that most divers who have been there will agree that Wakatobi has the best shore diving anywhere. Once you've shown the divemasters that you have a level of proficiency, you can dive from the shore at will; some folks may log five dives a day or even more.

You can easily get in as much diving as you might from a live-aboard, if not more. Many of the reefs begin in three feet of water, and you can have fabulous dives in very shallow water. I've come upon pygmy sea horses right off the beach, along with one of my favorite species, the comet longfin. I've seen frogfish in as little as six feet of water. It's wonderful for photographers, as you can try to capture shots of the same subject on numerous occasions, as many sites are simply so close to shore. For instance, there's fine a little family of spinecheek clownfish that I've been visiting for many years, right off the beach."

It's a long journey to reach Wakatobi (they joke that "It's not at the end of the earth, but you can see the end from here!"), but once you're there, you needn't travel far to find great sites. In fact, the reef that's right in front of the resort, less than a hundred yards away, is world class in every respect. "There is a great variety of fishes, invertebrates, macro subjects, beautiful soft corals, gorgonians, tunicates, whips, sponges, rays, overhangs, and beyond all else an unsurpassed rainbow of color," Ken continued. "In fact, the House Reef is so good that some of the first professional photographers who visited elected never to make a boat dive!" Fish species frequenting the House Reef include clownfish, batfish, crocodile fish, cuttlefish, several species of pygmy sea horses, and mandarin fish.

As difficult as it may be to pull oneself away from the House Reef and several adjoining sites (including Onamobaa Cavern, which has been likened to the famed Hanging Gardens at Sipadan), further wonders await a short boat ride away. "There's a wonderful variety of diving at Wakatobi, and many of the best boat dives are only fifteen or thirty minutes away," Ken said. "Wherever you go, you're conscious of the health of the reefs themselves." Some of Wakatobi's most renowned sites include Inka's Palette, Mari Mabuk, Turkey Beach, and Lorenz's Delight (named for lodge founder and proprietor Lorenz Maeder, a Swiss national who established the property in 1995). If he were to choose one site at Wakatobi to dive again and again, Ken might select Roma. "You start in bright rays of light in water as shallow as five feet, as large schools of fusiliers, pyramid butterfly, sergeant majors, hound fish, red-tooth triggerfish, and others swirl around you in an endless dance," Ken continued. "There's a compact pinnacle in the center of the reef, crammed with color and life. Banded sea snakes are common here and make exciting photo subjects.

"Another thing that impresses me each time I visit Wakatobi," Ken concluded, "is the incredible care that Lorenz and his staff take to protect the ecological system that they've come to love. Though the resort is hardly lacking for amenities—the kitchen is as sophisticated as anything you'd find in a European city—they've managed to limit their footprint."

KEN KNEZICK is founder and president of Island Dreams Travel (800-346-6116; www. divetrip.com). He has logged more than 3,000 scuba dives, at locations virtually all over the world, including Truk Lagoon, Palau, the Philippine Islands, the Red Sea, Malaysia, Indonesia, the Maldives, Fiji, the Solomon Islands, Vanuatu, New Caledonia, Costa Rica, Cocos, the Galápagos Islands, Hawaii, Mexico, the Caribbean, Sea of Cortez, Eastern and Western Europe, the Soviet Union, and Japan. He also has extensive experience as a divemaster in the Texas Gulf of Mexico, working as a divemaster aboard the M/V *Fling* and M/V *Spree*. A professional group-dive trip leader with more than twenty-five years' experience, Ken has led more than fifty dive groups to Cozumel alone. Since 1985, he has served as chairman of the Houston Underwater Club's Seaspace Exposition, is past president of Houston International Diver's Club, and a founding member of the Houston Underwater Photographic Society. He has presented seminars for Seaspace, Beneath the Sea, Our World Underwater, Ocean Expo, Scuba Show Long Beach, Boston Sea Rovers, and the Diving Equipment Manufacturers Association (DEMA). A graduate of Rutgers University and a member of Mensa, Ken has made Houston, Texas, his home since 1977. In 2002, he was inducted into the Scuba Schools International (SSI) Platinum Pro 5000 Society; in 2005, he was recipient of the PADI Project Aware/Seaspace Environmental Awareness Award.

IF YOU GO

➤ **Getting There**: You'll first need to reach Denpasar, Bali, which is served by Continental Airlines (via Hawaii and Guam), Singapore Airlines (via Singapore), and Cathay Pacific (via Hong Kong). From Denpasar, there is a charter flight to Wakatobi.

➤ **Best Time to Visit**: Prime times are between April and June and September and November. Diving can be quite good at other times, too; Wakatobi is closed during January and February, the rainy season.

➤ **Accommodations**: Wakatobi Dive Resort (www.wakatobi.com) is the only on-shore option at Wakatobi, but it's an excellent option with a friendly staff, great food, and a commitment to hard-core divers.

DESTINATION

22

PASSAMAQUODDY BAY

RECOMMENDED BY **Jonathan Bird**

On most house inspections, prospective owners are primarily concerned with the status of the furnace, whether the plumbing plumbs, and how sound the roof seems. When considering the purchase of a second home on Passamaquoddy Bay in Eastport, Maine, Jonathan Bird was more interested in meeting the neighbors. "It's the only home inspection I know of that involved a dive," he joked. "When the dive was finished, I was impressed enough to make an offer on the house. It was on that occasion that I met one of my oldest Eastport acquaintances, whom I came to know as Gene."

Gene, incidentally, is a wolf fish.

Passamaquoddy Bay lies off the easternmost tip of land in the United States, forming a border between Maine and New Brunswick. Technically an inlet of the Bay of Fundy, it stretches north from Eastport to St. Andrews, New Brunswick, where the St. Croix River empties into the salt. The bay is buffeted from the open water by two islands to the east: Campobello (site of Franklin Delano Roosevelt's famed summer retreat, now an international park) and Deer Island. The Bay of Fundy is renowned for some of the largest tides in the world, with a range of fifty-six feet between high and low. It's these extreme tides that help make Passamaquoddy Bay a special place to dive. "The currents—which can reach twelve knots—force-feed nutrients into the surrounding environs," Jonathan explained. "As a result, the invertebrate life is unlike anything else you'll find on the East Coast. People who've been diving around New England all of their lives come up here and can't believe they're still on the East Coast. While there's some of the same sea life you'll find south of here, everything is much bigger and more prevalent. Some refer to Passamaquoddy as the British Columbia of the east coast, and the two venues are quite similar in appearance."

OPPOSITE

Jonathan Bird's marine neighbor, Gene the wolf fish, smiles for the camera.

One of the highlights of diving in Passamaquoddy Bay is the opportunity to come upon tealia anemones in dizzying quantities. Tealias sustain themselves by capturing small fish and plankton with their tentacles and immobilizing their prey with venom; they take their name from the land flower they resemble. "Eastport is undoubtedly the tealia capital of the Atlantic," Jonathan said. "When one is found in the waters off Massachusetts, photographers line up to take pictures. There are probably more tealias per square foot on the bottom of Passamaquoddy Bay than anywhere else in the Atlantic; on a typical dive you could count 500 of them if you wanted to. You can find tealias in every color, including purple, and sometimes even yellow." Thanks to the region's cold waters ("Never over 52 degrees!" Jonathan added), a number of arctic invertebrates can also be found, including the horse star and winged sea star.

Most of your diving around Passamaquoddy Bay can be done from the shore. The drop-offs are very pronounced, so one seldom needs to venture far into the bay to find worthwhile sites. The dive schedule is pretty relaxed in "downeast" Maine, as the pronounced currents only permit diving during slack tides—that is, twice a day. While visibility wouldn't be characterized as superlative, it's reliable enough to keep most divers happy. "Often, you'll get a hurricane down south, and a few days later, visibility in the Atlantic off New England is zero—and I mean *zero*," Jonathan continued. "Thanks to how Eastport is set up, conditions in the bay never deteriorate to this level. Because of the tremendous currents and the amount of plankton cycling through, visibility is never great. Where I am, Campobello Island is only a mile across, and there's not enough fetch for wind to make a mess of things. It can be pouring rain, howling wind, there can be hurricanes down south, but visibility will always be fifteen feet; rarely good, rarely bad. The only time it's untenable is during scallop season, when the dredgers are working. But that's a small part of the year."

In addition to reliable (if limited) visibility and acres of tealias, visitors to Passamaquoddy Bay can count on encounters with *Anarhichas lupus*, the Atlantic wolf fish. These eel-like animals—equipped with caninelike choppers for crunching through the crustaceans that make up most of their diet—reside in small "dens" among rock beds, and are fairly common off Eastport. Some wolf fish will remain in the same quarters for years, like Gene, whom Jonathan Bird has visited with for eleven years (as of this writing).

"Gene frequents a den that's just off the beach from our cottage. A few other wolf fish have come and gone, but Gene's been consistent. A few years back, he was joined in a den nearby by another much larger specimen that we called Jack. We decided that the big wolf fish must be a male and that Gene must be a she—so we began calling her Jean. Jack left after three or four years, and Jean was by herself. We took to feeding her so we could get her to linger longer outside of her den, and we could get better pictures. Jean will eat urchins, but prefers whelks (a kind of snail). We'd take them out of the shell for her, and she came to expect it. We'd hold them farther and farther outside of the den, and she'd swim out around us to get them. Whenever we had a guest come down with us, Jean would come out. The diver would be frightened to death; we'd reassure them that it was just Jean, and she wants to be fed.

"Last summer, we took a few groups of divers up to Passamaquoddy to meet Jean. The first weekend, she came out on cue to eat and swim around us. The second weekend, she wouldn't come out. Eventually, I peeked into the den. There was the wolf fish, standing guard over a huge nest of eggs. Male wolf fish protect eggs, and it was this way that we realized that Jean was in fact Gene after all!"

JONATHAN BIRD is an Emmy Award–winning underwater cinematographer with experience in all aspects of underwater wildlife cinematography and still photography. He has shot and produced films for television that have aired all over the world. A frequent contributor to several diving magazines, and author of several books—including *Dolphins; Wildlife Monographs, Sharks; Wildlife Monographs, Dominica—Land of Water,* and *Adventures with Sharks.* Jonathan is also widely published on marine-life subjects. As president of the nonprofit environmental organization Oceanic Research Group, Inc., he produces educational films about marine life for use in schools and libraries, as well as satellite learning. He is a former professor in the broadcasting department at New England Institute of Art and Communications, in Boston, Massachusetts. He is currently in postproduction on his new high-definition documentary *Secrets of the Reef.*

IF YOU GO

➤ **Getting There**: Eastport is approximately 250 miles north of Portland, which is served by many major carriers, including Continental, Delta, and United Airlines. It's about 125 miles from Bangor, which is served by American, Continental, and Delta.
➤ **Best Time to Visit**: Visibility is acceptable except for scallop harvesting season, which

is December through April. Considering the normally chilly climes, most visit from late spring to early fall.

► **Accommodations**: Motel East (207-853-4747; moteleastport@prexar.com) is a popular lodging spot for visiting divers. Cabins are also available at Seaview Campground & Cabins (207-853-4471).

► **Dive Shops/Guides**: Eastport is lacking in dive shops/dive amenities. The nearest spot to get tanks filled is in Calais, nearly an hour away. Bottom line: Bring lots of full tanks! As for guides, Jonathan Bird leads several trips a year to Passamaquoddy; you can learn more at Jonathan Bird Productions (www.jonathanbird.net).

LAYANG LAYANG

RECOMMENDED BY **Simon Christopher**

Simon Christopher decided to establish Scubazoo near Sipadan, Malaysia, as the waters there are home to some of the world's greatest marine biodiversity. Given Simon's goals to communicate worthwhile conservation stories with Scubazoo's images, this seemed the very best place to start. When it was time to expand the organization's convervation mission and message, Layang Layang was the next stop. "It was a natural progression," Simon recalled. "Layang Layang is very unspoiled; there's been very little commercial fishing there, thanks to the proximity of the Malaysian navy. We strive to capture such pristine places on film so peole can understand what a healty marine ecosystem is like, and Layang Layang's near-perfect reef becomes more unique every day as other locations around the world are adversely affected by man's destructive fishing practices. I first dived there in 1997, and on the rare occasions I return, it's wonderful to see that the coral is as pristine as it was then and the marine life is just as abundant, too."

Layang Layang (pronounced "lie-young lie-young") is a smallish coral atoll that lies 200 miles northwest of the tip of Borneo in the South China Sea, off the Malaysian province of Sabah. It's one of the 600 islands that make up the Spratly chain. Layang Layang (which means "Swallows Reef" in Malay) was originally a series of thirteen interconnected coral reefs; the island, as it's expcrienced today, is largely the creation of the Malaysian government, which connected two reefs with extensive deposits of sand. A small naval base (averaging seventy residents) was established here in 1983, and soon after, a large dive resort (maximum capacity: 120 divers). The naval base was built in large part to strengthen Malaysia's territorial claim to the region; the dive resort, to take advantage of the incredible wall dives Layang Layang presents. Just off the island, the water plunges to depths of nearly 7,000 feet; this makes Layang Layang an ideal place to find large pelagics—most notably, hammerhead sharks.

111

"The first thing that strikes you about Layang Layang is its remoteness," Simon continued. "There's only one flight a day in. You wake up early and head to the airport at Kota Kinabalu, and there are ten other divers there yawning, and you know you're about to go on an adventure. The atoll is really in the middle of nowhere. There's a small airstrip, the naval station on the far side of the island, and the resort at the top of the atoll. You have incredible diving at each end of the atoll, and you feel like you're pushing the boundaries, as if you're exploring new frontiers. The visibility is staggering; on a good day, it can be nearly 200 feet. On many dives, you'll drop in on top of the reef, which can extend nearly to the surface in places. As you drop down, you'll come upon the reef fish you'd expect to find in Malaysia—bumphead parrotfish, barracuda, trevally, as well as grey reef and white-tip sharks. But the big draw at Layang Layang are the serious creatures that come up from the deep."

As mentioned above, the star pelagics here are the hammerhead sharks, which gather in large numbers from March through July. "At this time, you'll often see scalloped hammerheads by the hundreds," Simon added. "Sometimes they'll even be above the reef. I can recall looking up at a wall of coral and seeing a shape appear—the leader—and then watching the entire school of sharks make their way across. A religious experience!" It's not uncommon for hammerheads to gather in large schools, and marine biologists do not understand all the facets of this schooling behavior. However, at Layang Layang, schooling occurs because romance is in the water. The mating ritual unfolds something like this: females (which generally outnumber males by a factor of six) gather in the mid-section of the shoal, with the largest (and hence most sought after) females positioning themselves in the mid-section's core. Male sharks seek out the most desirable females, and as darkness descends they pair off to procreate. (To help gain purchase, males grab hold of the female with their teeth, leaving a lasting memento of the night's passion.)

In terms of big pelagics, hammerheads are only the beginning at Layang Layang. "You can drop in at Shark's Cave or Dog Tooth Lair, and you never know what might come past," Simon continued. "You get numerous cetaceans—spinner and bottlenose dolphins, pilot whales, and every year, pods of killer whales stop off on their migrations to feed on the hammerheads! You'll also get schools of devil rays circling the atoll. When you get wave after wave of pelagics coming through, everyone is in a daze."

Simon recounted an experience at Layang Layang that seems to capture the spirit of Scubazoo, and why the organization was formed. "When I and Jason Isley (cofounder of Scubazoo) first moved on to Layang Layang from Sipadan, we were very passionate about thresher sharks. We'd both seen threshers on our own, and as we were both filming, we were getting a little competitive to see who could get the best footage. On one dive, we went a bit deep to find them. Lo and behold, two thresher sharks came out of the depths. This was one of the high points of Scubazoo and it brought us back to the basics of why we were doing what we're doing—to create awareness about the oceans and help preserve creatures, like sharks and turtles, for future generations."

SIMON CHRISTOPHER is founder and CEO of Scubazoo (www.scubazoo.com), a team of professional underwater cameramen and photographers who have an intense love and appreciation of the marine world. After graduating from Swansea University, UK, with a B.Sc. (Hons) degree in zoology and spending four years in sales in London, he traveled extensively throughout Southeast Asia. During this time he developed his love of scuba diving. After becoming a PADI divemaster on Sipadan, Sabah, he left for Cairns, Australia, where he started his underwater filming career. In 1996, Simon returned to Sabah to start Scubazoo, with Jason Isley in hot pursuit. While continuously planning the growth and direction of the company, Simon now develops Scubazoo's broadcast opportunities. By accurately documenting this immensely fascinating and complex web of life—with mankind's intricate and vital link to it—Scubazoo's stories will always have a strong conservation message. Simon is a qualified PADI instructor with nitrox and videography specialties and has dived extensively throughout Southeast Asia, as well as the UK and South Africa.

IF YOU GO

➤ **Getting There**: Malaysia Airlines (www.malaysiaairlines.com) offers flights from Los Angeles to Kota Kinabalu, Malaysia. From here, a private airline (booked through Layang Layang Island Resort) will spirit you to Layang Layang.

➤ **Best Time to Visit**: March to August is the best time to visit, though good diving can be had a month on either end.

➤ **Accommodations**: The Layang Layang Island Resort (+603 2162-2877; www.layanglayang.com) is the only hotel and dive operator option on the island, but they have an excellent reputation. The Thailand-based operator Dive Master (+662 259-3191; www.divemaster.net) offers live-aboard excursions May through October.

SIPADAN

RECOMMENDED BY **Al Hornsby**

For Al Hornsby, Sipadan is a diving venue to which all the superlatives apply. "When I first heard about Sipadan in the mid-eighties—when Clement Lee from Borneo Divers had begun exploring the island from a diving point of view—it sounded like the kind of spot I'd love, a pristine place where very few people had been. I had two or three opportunities to go, but they all fell through. I finally got there in 1995, and have been back almost every year since. My wife learned to dive there one week while I was on an assignment. A year or so later, we went on a diving trip to another exotic and much-celebrated location. After the first dive, she made it clear that she was unimpressed. 'It's not like Sipadan,' was what she said."

Sipadan is a small island (roughly forty acres) situated about twenty miles off the northeast coast of Borneo in the Celebes Sea; the island is administered by the nation of Malaysia. It rises 2,000 feet from the ocean floor, and took form as coral grew upon the extinct volcanic cone. Sipadan's tremendous marine topography, plus its location in the heart of the Indo-Pacific basin, make it one of the world's richest diving habitats, with more than 3,000 fish species and hundreds of coral species scattered among a dozen well-established dive sites. Borneo Divers once operated a lodge on the island; in 2005, the island was declared a conservation zone and a UNESCO World Heritage site; the old lodge now serves as headquarters for officials overseeing Sipadan's protection. "Since the island was designated a protected park, you can already see a tremendous difference," Al added. "The more fragile corals are coming back, and the bigger fish are more prevalent. Divers are even starting to have encounters with whale sharks." Visitors are no longer permitted to overnight on the island. Instead, divers make day trips from nearby islands, most commonly Mabul.

OPPOSITE
A large school of oversized bumphead parrotfish resides around Sipadan, and when they come swimming by, you can hear the water being displaced by their fins.

"It takes a little while to get there," Al continued. "You can't see the island on the horizon from the mainland, which helps build your anticipation. When you do arrive, there's a stillness, a peacefulness, and sense of separation from the rest of the world. As for the diving, there just aren't any bad spots. A reef wall surrounds the entire island, and every place along the wall has interesting things to offer, whether it's gigantic gorgonian coral, immense schools of barracuda, legions of green and hawksbill turtles, or a huge group of outsize bumphead parrotfish—250 at least—that go thundering by like a herd of bison. At Sipadan, it feels as though Mother Nature has scooped up all it has to offer and dropped it down in one place."

Sipadan combines an astounding diversity of marine life with near-ideal conditions—calm warm seas, good visibility, and generally shallow and protected dive sites (though if one wishes to explore deeper terrain, the wall plunges nearly 2,000 feet in some places!). "Everyone from the most seasoned diver to the neophyte will find something to enjoy at Sipadan," Al continued. "And despite its remote location, logistics at Sipadan are very manageable. There are excellent dive operations at two nearby islands, Mabul and Kapalai. Everything is state-of-the-art in terms of boats and equipment, and accommodations are extremely nice."

There are at least a dozen dive sites around Sipadan that are noteworthy enough to have earned names, though two—Barracuda Point and Hanging Gardens—are at the top of Al Hornsby's "favorites" list. "Barracuda Point is one of those places where there's always something happening, though what's happening is always different, depending on the day. Gigantic schools of its namesake barracuda are virtually always there. Odds are that you've seen photographs of swirling schools of chevron barracuda with a diver in the middle; they were likely taken at Barracuda Point. The bumphead parrotfish come through, and you can actually hear them from the throbbing of their fins in the water. There are almost always turtles around, and white-tip sharks, too. When the current is pulling baitfish along the wall, you might even see bigger sharks and sailfish."

Hanging Gardens is another celebrated Sipadan site. Here, the wall descends in a series of terraces, festooned with gorgonian fans and *Dendronephythya alcyonarians* in a plethora of shades. (The name references the famed gardens of ancient Babylon, one of the Seven Wonders of the World.) "There are lush corals near the top," Al continued, "and many turtles, gray reef sharks, leaf scorpion fish, and many tropicals. Rivaling the barracuda of

Barracuda Point in terms of sheer numbers are the schools of horse-eye jack. There have been times when I've lain below such schools, and they were so compact that I couldn't see anything above them." Scalloped hammerheads and thresher sharks are sometimes viewed here in the open water off the wall.

In the ten-plus years that Al Hornsby has been visiting Sipadan, there have been many special moments. A stand-out is one of his encounters with the island's population of bump-head parrotfish. "The parrots are huge at Sipadan, three and four feet long. In other places in the Pacific you'll see them at times, but they're usually skittish, and certainly hard to photograph. That's not the case at Sipadan. As I mentioned earlier, during the day, they wander around in large schools. At night, in typical parrotfish fashion, they nest in holes on the reef wall. On one visit, I went on a night dive, and was able to witness this spectacle. As you go down the wall with your light, every nook and cranny has three or four parrotfish curled up, resting. The whole wall is covered with orange corals, encrusted sponges, and then every couple feet, a three-to-four-foot-long turquoise green bumphead, its mouth showing fused, beaklike teeth, perfect for chomping the coral. It's an absolutely unforgettable picture."

AL HORNSBY moved to the island of Guam with his family when he was twelve; the first time he put on a mask and slipped beneath the water's surface is still an indelible memory. The excitement he found underwater then has propelled him through life. After a stint as a photographer (doing both underwater work as well as racing, fashion, wildlife, and rock-'n'-roll), Al returned to diving, and eventually became a part of the early PADI (Professional Association of Diving Instructors) executive management team. He was also one of the developers of the environmental organization Project AWARE Foundation. Al served several years as editorial director at *Skin Diver* magazine, and returned to PADI a few years ago, as senior vice president of PADI Worldwide. He has served as president of the board for the dive industry trade association, DEMA. But all along, Al has continued writing about and photographing his diving adventures. Commuting now between Los Angeles and Singapore, he explores the incredible islands, reefs, and rainforests of the Asia Pacific region every available moment, discovering natural wonders that even forty years of diving adventure hasn't revealed before.

DESTINATION 25

➤ **Getting There**: Malaysia Airlines (www.malaysiaairlines.com) offers flights from Los Angeles to Kota Kinabalu, Malaysia, and then on to Tawau. From there, your resort will arrange ground transportation to the town of Semporna, where a boat will ferry you to your island destination—generally Mabul or Kapalai. Most Sipadan dive sites are twenty to twenty-five minutes away from the resorts.

➤ **Best Time to Visit**: Sipadan has excellent year-round conditions. There's some uncertain weather January through March, but conditions are still generally quite adequate.

➤ **Accommodations**: Sipadan has a number of excellent diving-oriented resorts. Al Hornsby recommends Sipadan Water Village (+60 89-75-2996; www.swvresort.com) and Borneo Divers Mabul Resort (+60 88-22-2226; www.borneodivers.info).

➤ **Dive Shops/Guides**: If you're not staying at a dive resort, Borneo Divers (+60 88-22-2226; www.borneodivers.info), which pioneered recreational diving at Sipadan, can provide background information.

DESTINATION

25

MALDIVES

RECOMMENDED BY **Duane Silverstein**

It was an interest in sea turtles that brought Duane Silverstein to the Maldives, though not in the way you might expect. "I work for a nonprofit called Seacology," Duane began, "and we work to preserve island cultures and environments around the globe. We do this by brokering agreements with islanders to curtail activities that are destructive to their local ecosystem in exchange for something tangible that their community needs.

"One day I was sitting in my office in Berkeley, California, and there was a call from the Four Seasons Resort in the Maldives. They were interested in sponsoring a project in the Maldives with Seacology. This first project concerned turtles, or, more accurately, turtle eggs. The Maldivian government had banned the taking of endangered turtles, but the regulation didn't ban the taking of eggs. The project that was proposed was that we build a preschool on the island of Kendhoo in exchange for an agreement by islanders to not take sea-turtle eggs. One way that Seacology raises money to fund such projects is to sponsor trips that introduce prospective donors to the project at hand. When they see how far our money goes, and how much is accomplished both for the environment and the quality of life of the local villagers, they almost always become donors. A small part of my job as director of Seacology is to take potential donors to such sites. That was how I first visited the Maldives."

The Republic of the Maldives consists of twenty-six coral atolls and 1,200 islets, roughly 400 miles southwest of the southern tip of India. The landmass of the Maldives stretches some 500 miles from Tiladummati Atoll in the north to Addu Atoll in the south, and encompasses some 56,000 square miles of the Indian Ocean; the average elevation of this nation of atolls and islands is just north of three feet above sea level, making it the world's flattest republic. Thanks to their isolated location and the strong currents that whip through, the Maldives are one of the globe's biomass capitals. "If you're not a diver and

you're sitting at home watching a Jacques Cousteau special, you'd think that on your average dive—wherever it might be—you'd see thousands of fish," Duane continued. "That's not true anymore. You don't have many sites where you're overwhelmed with pure numbers of fish, but this is still a regular occurrence in the Maldives. I remember one dive site in particular, a wreck called the *Kudhimaa*. The wreck itself was not very interesting, but there were so many glassfish that no one in my group could come up with an accurate estimate. It was a special experience to be swimming in the midst of tens or even hundreds of thousands of fish. You encounter such tremendous numbers of fish at many other sites as well." In addition to great numbers of fish, the Maldives serve up excellent biodiversity, with upward of 700 fish species and more than 10,000 invertebrate species.

"Another attraction of Maldives diving is the chance you have of running into charismatic pelagics," Duane said. "We went to a place called Manta Point (*Lankanfinolhu Faru* in Maldivian parlance) for a morning dive, after our divemasters pronounced that it was the best place in the Maldives to see mantas. That morning, we saw zero. The divemaster wanted to move elsewhere, but we'd come pretty far to get to Manta Point, and we said we wanted to stay for another dive. We headed back down, and it was manta-ray heaven. Giant specimens came by, with fifteen- to sixteen-foot wingspans. They were so close we could have touched them. It was almost as if they were putting on a show for us, doing 'loop the loops' in pairs. It was a transcendental experience, both for the interaction with the rays, and the interaction with my fellow divers. I could see people's expressions, even through their masks. Their beatific smiles made that dive quite memorable." (Mantas visit Lankanfinolhu Faru from the deep water thanks to the presence of "cleaner fish" like Napoleon wrasse, who live in porites corals around the site. In a lovely symbiotic interaction, the mantas hover over the coral and the cleaner fish nibble parasites off the rays' skin.)

While there are a number of land-based resorts that cater to divers, visitors to such operations are limited to diving at nearby reefs (roughly eighty islands have tourist developments). "For serious divers," Duane added, "a live-aboard is the only way to go. Sites are spread over thousands of miles, and the mothership puts them all within reach. As live-aboards go, the Four Seasons *Explorer* is unrivaled in terms of luxury—if one can afford it!" Most diving is done from *dhonis*, forty- to forty-five-foot local fishing boats launched from the mothership. Diving terrain around this atoll-riddled region can be divided into four types: *thila*s (submerged pinnacles inside the atoll); *giri*s (areas of coral smaller than a *thila* and also found within the atoll); *kandu*s (channels through the atoll rim); and *faru*s (circular

*OPPOSITE
Longfin
bannerfish, part
of the Maldives'
rich piscine
bounty.*

DESTINATION

26

121

reefs generally resting in ocean channels). When diving in a *kandu* or outside an atoll, you'll want (or be required) to use a safety sausage, lest the strong currents sweep you away from your group. During the southwest monsoon (spring) season, visibility can be up to 130 feet; during the northeast monsoon (fall), it can rise to 200 feet.

"As great as the diving is in the Maldives, the highlight from a recent trip was visiting the Seacology-funded preschool in Kendhoo that was built as part of our project," Duane added. "Everyone on the ship went along to the school, and we were greeted by the entire population of the island, who wanted to show their gratitude. It was hard not to cry."

DUANE SILVERSTEIN is executive director of Seacology (www.seacology.org). For twenty years prior to heading Seacology he was the executive director of the Goldman Fund, one of California's largest philanthropic foundations. He also headed the Goldman Environmental Prize, which has been dubbed the "Nobel Prize of the Environment" by *National Geographic*. Duane has met with many presidents of the United States, secretaries-general of the United Nations, and heads of state throughout the world. His work has been covered in newspapers and periodicals as diverse as *Time*, the *Bangkok Post*, the *San Francisco Chronicle*, and *Rodale's Scuba Diving* magazine. Articles he has written have appeared in *Asian Geographic*, *Fathoms*, and *Asian Diver*, among many other newspapers and magazines. The *New York Times* has called Silverstein "one of the world's leading island explorers." He is a National Fellow of the Explorers Club.

IF YOU GO

➤ **Getting There**: Male, the main island of the Maldives, is served by Qatar Airways (877-777-2827; www.qatarairways.com) and Emirates (800-777-3999; www.emirates.com).

➤ **Best Time to Visit**: June to October and December to March are recommended, though conditions around the Maldives permit diving year round.

➤ **Accommodations**: While nearly all the resorts around the Maldives offer diving, serious divers generally opt for a live-aboard. Duane stayed on the Four Seasons *Explorer* (800-819-5053; www.fourseasons.com/maldives; Dive the World Liveaboards (+66 83-505-7794; www.divetheworldliveaboards.com) lists a number of other options.

BIKINI ATOLL

RECOMMENDED BY **Doug Toth**

Fifty years ago, few would have thought of setting foot on Bikini Atoll, let alone diving there. But from the dust and detritus of more than twenty nuclear-weapons tests, the lagoon at Bikini Atoll has emerged as one of the Pacific's greatest wreck-diving sites.

"I first heard about Bikini from a writer/photographer friend, Eric Hanauer, who had made a trip there when Bikini first opened up for diving," Doug Toth recalled. "Eric wanted to make another trip so he could dive again with the divemaster (Fabio Amaral) who'd pioneered the dive operation there, as he was retiring. My wife and I decided to tag along. I must admit that I didn't know a lot about Bikini. I'd heard that there was some excellent wreck diving, including an aircraft carrier. The history of the place intrigued me, especially as I read up on it."

Bikini Atoll indeed has a rich, if at times ignominious, history. The atoll (a mass of coral that encircles a lagoon) comprises twenty-three separate islands and a 240-square-mile lagoon, and is situated in the central Pacific, roughly 2,200 miles southwest of Honolulu. While the larger Marshall Islands were explored by Spaniards and Germans, who saw potential for the production of copra oil (from coconuts), Bikini Atoll's more isolated location and dry climate discouraged any colonization... that is, until the Japanese military established a watchtower on the island at the outset of Japan's entrance into World War II. While Bikini and its 200-odd citizens were spared combat, they eventually faced displacement when it was decided that their home would become the site of weapons testing to, in President Harry Truman's words, "determine the effect of atomic bombs on American warships." Concurrent with the onset of testing, it had been determined that Bikini Lagoon would become the final resting place of a number of vessels from the US fleet, including the USS *Saratoga*, an aircraft carrier; and the much-maligned *Nagato*, flagship of the Japanese navy

in 1941, when Admiral Isoroku Yamamoto and his staff planned the Pearl Harbor attack. In 1946, the first of twenty-three nuclear bombings was conducted. Early tests included the famously photographed BAKER blast, which ultimately sank both the *Saratoga* and the *Nagato*.

For nearly forty years after the last test bombing in 1958, Bikini Atoll was off limits for visitors. In 1996, however, the lagoon was opened to limited recreational diving and sport fishing by a coalition of islanders and outside operators who were brought in for their expertise in tourist operations. (The islanders have control of the tourism operation; it's hoped that revenues from tourism will ultimately allow displaced generations of Bikini islanders to return there to live, as lingering radiation has made their former agricultural/fishing way of life impossible.) "The diving operation is fabulous," Doug said. "For those not experienced with wreck diving it can be intimidating, especially as these are mostly deep, long decompression dives, one hundred to 190 feet. But everything is so well planned out, and there's so much preparation before each dive, that you're made to feel very comfortable. And it doesn't hurt that there are bathtub-like conditions—warm all the time, no current, no surf, and very clear."

The dive program at Bikini Atoll has a fittingly military regimentation. Guests visit for seven nights, and over the course of their stay, take twelve dives, ranging from sixty to 110 minutes. A number of craft are visited, including the USS *Lamson* (a destroyer), the USS *Arkansas* (a battleship), and the USS *Apogon* (a submarine). For wreck enthusiasts, the focal point of the trip is the aircraft carrier *Saratoga*. "The *Saratoga* is the first dive, which occurs on the day you arrive," Doug continued. "In the pre-dive briefing, you get a detailed review of the ship itself. They even have little plastic models of the ship, so they can illustrate exactly where you're going to begin and end your dive, and what you're going to see. (A series of films is also shown in the course of the week, to give visitors a historical context for what they're experiencing.) Soon after, you're in a boat, heading out to the dive site. The *Saratoga* dive is one of the shallower dives, about a hundred feet or so. From the surface, you can see the carrier. The immensity of the craft is overwhelming."

Initially designed as a Lexington-class battle cruiser, the *Saratoga* was constructed by the New York Shipbuilding Company between 1920 and 1925. The *"Sara"* was commissioned in 1927, and at 880 feet in length and nearly 40,000 tons in weight, is the largest divable ship in the world as well as the only divable aircraft carrier. Visitors to Bikini Lagoon can access several points of interest on the *Saratoga*, including the bridge, the flight

OPPOSITE
A diver inspects the bridge of the USS Anderson, a destroyer sacrificed in the nuclear testing at Bikini Atoll.

DESTINATION

27

deck, and the hangar, where her planes—Helldiver bombers—waited for action. Several Helldivers and their 500-pound bombs remain on display. "The dive to the hangar is one of the highlights of the trip," Doug continued. "You're within the interior of the ship, and it's a huge, huge space. The divemasters guide you through with lights, pointing out facets of the planes and the ship. It's fascinating.

"There are so many wrecks in close proximity at Bikini, all in this big fishbowl," Doug added. "When you see these ships, you can't help but imagine what it must have been like to be on them when they were above water. What it must have been like to watch them being sunk, what it must have been like to witness the detonation of the nuclear bombs. One of the biggest surprises I had on the trip was my wife Bonnie's response to the experience. Typically, she has little interest in war history; I think this tends to be more of a male thing. She really enjoyed discovering the history of the ships and the tests at Bikini Atoll, and seeing them firsthand brought all that history back to life."

DOUG TOTH is cofounder and co-owner (with Dean Garraffa) of Atomic Aquatics (www. atomicaquatics.com), which markets a range of innovative diving products, including the world's first titanium regulator. Trained as a marine biologist, Doug worked as a dive instructor part-time before eventually turning his interests to mechanical design, and the creation of dive equipment. "I've never forgotten how much more difficult it was to train new divers with equipment that was overly complicated, uncomfortable, or difficult to use," Doug said. "Reliability and safety are expected, but the gear should also be simple, functional, and fun to use—and that's our goal."

IF YOU GO

➤ **Getting There**: Bikini Atoll is reached via Majuro, Marshall Islands, on Air Marshall Islands (69 26-25-3731; www.airmarshallislands.com). Majuro is served via Honolulu on Continental Airlines.

➤ **Best Time to Visit**: Bikini Atoll is open for diving from March through November.

➤ **Accommodations**: Bikini Atoll Diving (+69 26-25-3177; www.bikiniatoll.com) is the sole operator on Bikini Atoll.

AKUMAL

RECOMMENDED BY **Roxanne Pennington**

For many divers, Mexico's Yucatán Peninsula conjures up images of the shimmering green waters of the western Caribbean and Cozumel, with perhaps a sidelong glance at the ruins of Tulum. For Roxanne Pennington, the Yucatán means *cenotes*.

"Outside of Akumal, Mexico, there are underwater caverns that the Mayans believed were sacred," Roxanne began. "The water is crystal clear and the views of the stalactites and stalagmites are spectacular. As light shines through openings, it creates a beam with incredible colors. When you surface and see and hear the jungle, it's breathtaking."

Cenotes (pronounced "say-no-tays") are a geological phenomenon found through much of the state of Quintana Roo, on the eastern side of the Yucatán peninsula. The story of how cenotes came to be so prevalent in the region is fairly complex, but in short form goes like this: The surface strata consists of porous limestone, remnants of what was not so long ago (in geologic terms) an ocean floor. Over thousands of years, rainwater filtered through the limestone, creating an extensive series of underground rivers, with accompanying caverns. Cenotes are essentially sinkholes that occur when the limestone surface crumbles. The Mayans revered cenotes, viewing them as portals to a spiritual world below the earth. (At the ruins of Chichén Itzá, northwest of Akumal, divers have discovered jewelry, pottery, and human skeletons, believed to be offerings to the gods; it's uncertain whether the skeletons were the result of human sacrifice by drowning.) On a pragmatic day-to-day basis, cenotes were extremely important to eastern Yucatán residents as a source of fresh water for drinking and irrigation. Some cities were constructed around cenotes to facilitate easy access to fresh water.

Today, cenotes give casual passersby a wonderful spot to take a cooling freshwater plunge, snorkelers an interesting chamber to inspect, and divers an entrance to a vast

underwater cave system. "Among my diving experiences, visiting the cenotes is a one-of-a-kind experience, in many ways," Roxanne continued. "It starts with the adventure of getting there—by land instead of by boat. Most of the cenotes are marked by signs along the main road. You pay a small entrance fee to access the cenote in question, then go bumping along a rugged road, back into the jungle—the sound of clanking equipment in the back of the jeep or van stays with me. Eventually, you reach a parking area, where there's a table where you can gear up. From the start, you have the feeling that this isn't going to be your normal dive!

"Once you're geared up, you walk down a path, or some stairs or a wooden ladder, to the water. Each cenote has its own type of entry, which is part of its individual charm. The water is cool and exhilarating—around 75 degrees—so you might need a wet suit, though the local guides dive in their swimsuits. When you enter the water, but before you go under, you're struck by the sounds of the jungle—the calls of the monkeys and mot mots. When you go under, the water is so clear that you can barely tell you're under water. (Visibility in some cenotes can reach 350 feet.) As you submerge, you see all the different colors of the various limestone formations—stalactites, stalagmites. As you swim along, there will be beams of light coming through from the cenote. On most dives, a third or halfway through, there will be an open room with part of the area above water. When you surface, it's silent except for the sounds of the birds. Some of these rooms let you see the open greenery. It's an inspiring experience to be floating there in the midst of this unspoiled wilderness. It's where I'd like to go when I die—the play of light, the music of nature, all coupled with my love of diving."

Cenote diving has some protocols and techniques that are its own. Like for night diving, participants are outfitted with flashlights to light the way through the tunnels and caverns. Divers need to have a good sense of buoyancy to control how fast they ascend and descend. "You don't want to bump into a stalactite or stalagmite," Roxanne added. "First, it took a long time for these to grow, and you want to be respectful. And second, it would hurt—on one occasion, a diver we were with pushed the inflate button by accident, and he nearly impaled himself on a stalagmite. You also need to use a modified kick, so you don't stir up sediment on the bottom and diminish visibility. One odd experience in cenote diving is the haloclines that occur when salt water seeping in from the ocean and the fresh water of the underground river mingle. Where the higher density salt water meets the fresh—at about thirty-five feet—visibility is blurred. It's like looking through an oil slick, though visibility is fine above and below." Divers are advised to always stay in sight of sunlight, though there are guidelines that track through the cenote.

OPPOSITE
The cenotes around Akumal on the Yucatán Peninsula provide a one-of-a-kind cave diving experience.

DESTINATION

28

There are many cenotes to choose from, and new ones are identified each year after heavy rainstorms. Many are named. "Each cenote has different colors and configurations," Roxanne said. "Car Wash is one that many people start with. It's very pool-like, easy to get into, and easy to navigate around. (Local people used to wash their cars here, hence the name.) The limestone of Gran Cenote is completely white, which is very cool in itself. Most of the cenotes are thirty to seventy feet deep; Dos Ojos, which is featured in an IMAX movie, is 351 feet deep, and has bats in one of the caverns. One that stands out for me is Temple of Doom, I think because the entry requires a ten-foot jump. I was the first girl to go in from our group, as I knew I'd chicken out if I didn't go quickly!"

Should one tire of the cenotes, rumor has it that the open waters off Akumal are home to some pretty good diving, too!

ROXANNE PENNINGTON is co-owner of DiveTravel.com, Inc. (www.divetravel.com), and a travel writer, photographer, and videographer. Roxanne began her travel career in 1982 and earned the Certified Travel Counselor (CTC) designation from the Travel Institute (formally The Institute of Certified Travel Agents) in 1989. Roxanne was certified to scuba dive in 1994 and has since earned the Master Diver Certification, Cavern Diver, and NITROX certifications. Her dive travels have taken her all over the world.

IF YOU GO

➤ **Getting There**: Akumal is about one-and-a-half hours' drive from the Cancún International Airport, which is served by many major carriers.

➤ **Best Time to Visit**: You can dive the cenotes year round, though summers are uncomfortably warm for most tastes, and there's always the chance of hurricanes in the early fall. March and April are the driest months.

➤ **Accommodations**: Akumal offers a broad array of accommodations, from modest *palapas* on the beach to all-inclusive resorts, to rental homes. LocoGringo.com provides a good overview of options.

➤ **Dive Shops/Guides**: A number of outfitters lead cenote dives; they're listed on LocoGringo. com. NOTE: A guide is required for cavern diving unless you are cavern certified.

ISLA GUADALUPE

RECOMMENDED BY **Patric Douglas**

Patric Douglas had never thought much about great white sharks—let alone diving with them. But after his first encounter, he was hooked. "I was running a company leading people on outdoor-oriented adventures," Patric began, "and accompanied a fellow who was taking guests on shark-viewing expeditions off the Farallon Islands, west of San Francisco. We were towing a seal decoy in the fog and cold, not quite knowing what to expect, when a magnificent eighteen-footer came blasting out of the water. It makes an impression on you. At that moment I knew that sharks, and shark diving, were going to be a huge part of my life.

"Back in 1998, we began hearing reports from tuna fishermen who were encountering large numbers of sharks off Isla Guadalupe, which is roughly 210 miles southwest of San Diego," Patric continued. "They were coming up and taking 200-pound yellowfin tuna right at the boat off anglers' lines. An expedition with Doc Anes went there in 2001 and dropped a shark cage in the water. Two hours later, there were four great whites around the divers in water with one hundred feet of visibility. South Africa was the current hotspot for great white sharks at the time, but with the sheer numbers of animals we encountered off Isla Guadalupe, I knew we had something special."

Isla Guadalupe is a volcanic island that's ninety square miles in size. It was used as a provisioning station for Russian whalers and sealers in the early 1800s; today it's populated by a handful of abalone and lobster fishermen, and by shark researchers from UC Davis and Cicimar (The Centro Interdisciplinario de Ciencias Marinas). Scientists are convinced that the sharks that return to Isla Guadalupe to feed on the abundant tuna and endemic Guadalupe fur seals each fall spend most of the year in the deep waters of the central Pacific, where they're joined by the sharks that frequent Año Nuevo and the Farallons. Satellite tagging suggests that the same sharks return to the same feeding grounds each year.

Great white sharks are the undisputed apex predators of the ichthyological world; only killer whales, humans (albeit well-armed humans), and other white sharks pose the creatures any danger. Specimens of *Carcharodon carcharias* surpassing twenty-five feet have been reported, though fish of twelve to sixteen feet reaching weights ranging from 2,000 to 2,500 pounds are more typical. Great whites can eat just about whatever they wish, with the menu including large fish and whale carcasses. Given their druthers, however, they seem to prefer to feed on members of the pinniped family—fur seals, sea lions, and elephant seals. (Attacks on humans—especially surfers—are often attributed to mistaken identity; from below, a surfboard or wet-suited person may resemble a sea lion.) Great whites can be found through most of the oceans of the world, sometimes swimming to depths of 4,000 feet. Satellite tagging has shown that individual fish will often range thousands of miles in the course of a year (in one study, a shark was shown to have traveled over 12,000 miles in nine months!). While Steven Spielberg's shark menaced swimmers on fictional Amity Island (filmed on Nantucket), great whites are found in greatest concentrations in the waters off South Africa, along the southern coast of Australia, and in the Pacific off California and around Isla Guadalupe.

The cages that make Isla Guadalupe shark diving possible are designed of one-inch by one-inch aluminum bars, with a 5,000-pound crush strength; they're built to withstand the impact of a curious great white who decides he/she needs a closer look at you. Divers are divided into teams of four, and groups will cycle through the cages all day. Shark interactions are virtually guaranteed during each dive; on some occasions, divers have been treated to as many as seven different animals on one rotation.

Patric Douglas and his team have helped identify 160 animals that visit their cages regularly—sometimes within a few hundred yards of shore. Many have earned names. "We call one shark Scarboard," Patric said, "as this female has big scars along her right side. We can always identify Scarboard as she's flanked by pilot fish that follow her everywhere; whenever the pilot fish appear, we know Scarboard is not far behind. Another frequent visitor is Shredder, who earned his name dubiously during our first season out there. I was in the wheelhouse with the boat's captain Greg Grivetto when there was a tremendous splash off the bow. We looked down to see one of our clients looking up at us and his face was as white as a sheet. I thought someone had fallen in. The client shouted up, 'The biggest shark I've ever seen just blasted out of the water and severed your anchor cable, and you're adrift!' Greg, who was standing next to me, said 'No way.' After all, the cable is as thick as your

OPPOSITE
Those who venture to Isla Guadalupe are almost certain to see white sharks on each dive— from the safety of aluminum cages.

DESTINATION

29

133

arm, designed to hold a one-hundred-foot boat in place in all kinds of weather conditions. A crew member soon appeared and pulled in what was left of that cable, absolutely shredded. A biologist who does white shark research with us has theorized that Shredder may have thought that our boat was a large whale, and that the rope was an intestine—the first morsel that sharks like to feed on when they come upon a rotting whale carcass."

One of Isla Guadalupe's regulars, "Fat Tony," earned his moniker from what Patric described as his bullying, Mafioso ways. "Fat Tony likes to tail slap the cage from the bottom," Patric said. "We don't know for certain why he does this, but we believe that he understands that the creatures inside the cage do react, and he's looking for a reaction. While some sharks don't seem to take any interest in the divers in the cage, others do. Even more spooky, there are times when a shark seems to focus on a particular diver. The shark's eyeball rotates; when it locks on an individual, it stays focused on that diver as the shark swims past until it's almost halfway around in the socket. When the eye locks on you, everything else in the world disappears—it's just you and that shark. It's quite a feeling when a predator as fearsome as a white shark is that close and has taken an interest in you."

PATRIC DOUGLAS has worked in the travel industry for the past eighteen years, leading adventure-oriented tours to Vietnam, China, Bali, Australia, New Zealand, and Latin America, among other places. He launched SharkDiver.com in 2000; the company leads other shark-oriented expeditions in the Bahamas and worldwide. Shark Diver has been featured on the National Geographic Channel and the Discovery Channel, among many other media outlets; they regularly guide film crews and private clients from around the world.

IF YOU GO

➤ **Getting There**: Isla Guadalupe is roughly 210 miles southwest of San Diego.
➤ **Best Time to Visit**: Great whites are present off Isla Guadalupe from August through November.
➤ **Guides/Accommodations**: Trips are led by several outfitters, including Patric's company, Shark Diver (888-405-3268; www.sharkdiver.com).

SANTA ROSALIA

RECOMMENDED BY **Scott Cassell**

The Sea of Cortez is renowned for its great concentrations of whales in the late winter and spring. For Scott Cassell, it is the squid—more specifically *Dosidicus gigas*, or the Humboldt Squid—that draws him south to Baja California. "Anyone can swim in clear water and see pretty fish," Scott began. "I'm first and foremost a research scientist and explorer, and I seek out difficult expeditions. This certainly qualifies. These squid, which can grow to 250 pounds (and perhaps much more), will try to attack and kill a human being in certain settings. I've been swimming with and filming these animals for thirteen years, they fascinate me. My desire is to spread the word about what these animals are like, and capture people's imagination. I'm getting more and more people who want to dive with me to experience these squid—though I don't see myself leading tours, as much as allowing people to tag along with me."

The Humboldt Squid takes its name from Humboldt Current off Peru, where the animal was first discovered. Their nickname is *Demonio Rojo* or red demon. They can measure 7 feet and more, with their body (which contains the animals' internal organs, including 3 hearts, and large eyes for night vision) making up a little over half their length, and their eight arms and two tentacles making up their remainder. Each arm has anywhere between 150–200 suction discs, each equipped with a chitenous ring that can have anywhere between 15–30 very sharp teeth. They capture prey—commonly including other Humboldt Squid—by wrapping their arms around the creature in question and biting and ripping at it with their chitenous ring teeth and beak. (Researchers have repeatedly watched hordes of squid viciously turn on a fellow squid which has been hooked by a fisherman or otherwise injured.) Their bodies, incidentally are not actually red; the squid's skin is transparent and their muscle underneath is white with red pigmented tissue. They have thousands of

chromatophors that open and close individually. When the chromatophors open they show the color red and when they close they show white.

Red demon squid range through much of the eastern Pacific, from the tip of South America to California and even on to Alaska. Numbers have proliferated in the Sea of Cortez in recent years; Scott and other scientists attribute this to the decline of predators like shark and marlin. Generally traveling in large schools of up to 1,000 specimens, red demons spend most of their time at depths of 600 feet or more. Scott puts this cephalopod in a most chilling perspective: "They are eleven times stronger than you, and are as smart as a dog or smarter. They're a few feet away, and they're wondering how they can eat you. It's an alien-like encounter."

Scott's very first meeting was more likened to a mugging. "In short, I got my ass handed to me by some squid. I had heard about red demons while I was filming gray whales at Laguna San Ignacio. I went south to La Paz to dive under some of the squid-fishing fleets. Soon I was surrounded by squid. One smashed my camera into my face. Another wrapped itself around my head and yanked my right arm out of its socket. Meanwhile, a third bit into my chest, and the group dragged me down forty feet in a matter of seconds, rupturing my eardrum in the process. I managed to free myself and get to the surface. I still have scars on my throat and the side of my face from that encounter. I realized I had to figure out a way to be able to be close enough to film them while being protected. I was inspired by the armor the stormtrooper characters wore in *Star Wars*. I contacted Lucas Films, and they sent along the molds. I filled them with fiberglass (and later lined them with Kevlar), and they worked pretty well—that is, until the squid realized there was no armor on the knees and elbows. Soon after, I met Jeremiah Sullivan, a leading shark researcher, and together we developed the armor I use today, a variation on a standard shark suit that's strong enough to deflect the animal's beak."

Gaining a firsthand understanding of the red demons is not something people do casually on their own. Scott has developed a crash course in interacting with Humboldts—the Squid School. "The first day when people come down to Santa Rosalia (where the squid are not fished and hence we can observe their natural behavior), we go out and have dinner to get acquainted. The next day, we give an interactive presentation that covers the Sea of Cortez and the anatomy and physiology of squid. I show guests film of the animals in motion, including some footage of what it's like to be attacked. Next I introduce the armor. Guests then try it on for size, and we snap some pictures. Then we move on to explain our

*OPPOSITE
Smarter than a
dog and 11 times
stronger than a
man, red demon
squid demand
extreme respect.*

DESTINATION

30

cable suspension system. Once you understand how the armor works and how we position ourselves in the water (usually at a depth of forty feet), you can focus on the behavioral aspects of this alien." The protocol of squid diving is simple: Once divers reach forty feet and are clipped on to the suspension cable, someone on deck drops an attraction device (like a jig) to a depth of 500 or 600 feet. The jigger can feel when squid are on the device, and as the attractor is drawn toward the surface, the squid follow . . . and the show begins. (Assuming you don't find yourself in the midst of a feeding frenzy, the chances of an attack are low; none of Scott's guests has ever been victimized.)

To film squid at extreme depths, Scott has captured a red demon in the morning, attached a critter cam on a micro tether, and released the creature. At the end of the day he brings the animal in and retrieves the camera to review the footage. "With my squid cam, I've seen the delicate side of these incredible predators—the mating and courting," he added. "They are very delicate, deliberate, and gentle. I was awestruck with the consideration these animals showed for each other. It was especially jarring, given that in the previous decade I'd only seen their problem-solving intelligence in order to feed, and their potential for ferocity."

SCOTT CASSELL has been diving since 1977, accumulating more than 12,000 hours of dive time. He is a rated mixed-gas commercial diver, explorer-filmmaker, a 20-year veteran of Closed Circuit Rebreather technology, and a USCG qualified Submersible Pilot. He was the first person in history to film the giant squid in its natural environment, a 35 to 40 foot long animal weighing up to 1,800 lbs, free swimming in predatory behavior, which was debuted in the History Channel's *Monster Quest—Giant Squid: FOUND*. Scott holds the world record for Longest Distance Traveled by a Diver (52 miles in 9.5 hours nonstop saturation dive). He used a diver tow-glider he invented to cover more range for open-sea underwater filming. An Advanced Diving Medical Technician Instructor (1 of 10 in the USA), Commercial Diving Instructor, and Hyperbaric Medical Technician Instructor, Scott taught for years at the College Of Oceaneering. He is also a PADI Instructor. Scott is featured as "on-screen talent" with MTV's WILDBOYZ. His work with giant Humboldt Squid has been featured on over six Discovery Channel productions, The History Channel, Animal Planet, and the BBC, not to mention Disney's *20,000 Leagues Under the Sea* DVD where his work on Humboldt Squid is featured on a bonus track. A U.S. Navy qualified Diving Supervisor and

Dive Medical Technologist; Scott has worked in Maritime Counter Terrorism Operations for client companies where his secret operations often involved "High Risk" world regions.

IF YOU GO

➤ **Getting There**: Scott Cassell (and his partner, Shawna Meyer) base their expeditions out of Santa Rosalia, Mexico. Limited flights from the U.S. are available to nearby Loreto through Aeromexico (800-237-6639; www.aeromexico.com).

➤ **Best Time to Visit**: For now, you need Scott to dive with the red demons, and they're leading limited expeditions from March through October.

➤ **Accommodations**: The Las Casitas Hotel (www.santarosaliacasitas.com) is the accommodation of choice for expeditions led by SquidDiving.com.

➤ **Dive Shops/Guides**: Red demon expeditions are orchestrated by SquidDiving.com (760-280-9556; www.squiddiving.com), and generally consist of a five-day/four-night itinerary. Baja California certainly has attractions to hold you there longer.

DESTINATION

30

SOCORRO ISLAND

RECOMMENDED BY **Mark Talkovic**

"Growing up and learning to dive in California, it's somewhat rare to come upon something large when you're in the water—let alone close up!" Mark Talkovic began. "And if you do, your instinct is that 'big' means 'scary and hungry.' This is not the case with the giant manta rays of Socorro Island."

Socorro Island is located roughly 250 miles south of Cabo San Lucas, off the southern tip of Baja California. It's the largest of the Revillagigedo islands at fifty square miles; another desirable diving venue in the Revillagigedos is San Benedicto. The first European encounter with uninhabited Socorro came in the early 1500s when Spanish explorers came upon the island and named it Saint Thomas. The island went through a few more name changes before it was dubbed Socorro—or "Help"—in 1608; the name that stuck speaks to Socorro's isolation. "The islands are of a volcanic nature, rising up abruptly from the ocean floor with steep sides," Mark continued. (Socorro is still the site of volcanic activity, the last eruption occurring in 1993.) "You can be a hundred yards off shore and find yourself in 500 feet of water. The structure in this isolated stretch of ocean brings in many big pelagics, including the mantas. On some days of diving, we had manta rays racing around like dogs in a city park. Some would follow you around like puppies!" (Some think that the manta's companionable behavior toward divers may be attributable to mistaken identity; mantas may view humans as giant cleaner fish!)

Mark arrived at Socorro at the conclusion of an expedition to hone his newly minted photography skills. "I had just finished the undersea photo program at the Brooks Institute of Photography, out on an Alaska purse seiner that they had retrofitted to be a floating classroom, the *Just Love*," Mark explained. "We traveled south, from Santa Barbara, California, down along Baja, gunk holing in anywhere we could and diving all along the way. Eventually

OPPOSITE
One of Socorro's
oversized mantas
pirouettes for a
visitor.

we ended up at Socorro. I've been back two other times. Some refer to Socorro as the Mexican Galápagos, as there are a number of endemic terrestrial plant and animal species here. Socorro is fairly lush with greenery; San Benedicto, just fifteen miles away, is like the surface of the moon. The contrast is startling. While there's a small Mexican naval station on the island, there are no tourist accommodations; it's a live-aboard situation, and it's a solid day or two run to get there."

With their expansive "wings" (pectoral fins) and graceful pirouettes, manta rays are one of the tropical seas' megacharismatic species. The largest member of the ray family, mantas can reach lengths of twelve feet and more, widths of nearly twenty feet, and a weight of over 5,000 pounds. Despite their tremendous size, they are extremely docile creatures, subsisting on plankton and small fish, which they direct into their expansive mouths with their distinctive "horns." There are several diving venues around the world where manta encounters are quite reliable—Kona, Hawaii's, famous night dives, and Yap in Micronesia come to mind—but for consistent exposure to very large mantas, Socorro may be tough to beat. "During three weeks at Socorro, we saw at least one manta ray on 75 percent of our dives," Mark said. "At a couple of spots where the rays come in to be cleaned by reef fish, you might see six or seven at a glance. They'll swim by these large submerged rocks, then stall and hover, and reef fish will come out and clean them. It takes next to no effort on the diver's part; all you have to do is sit and wait, and you're only fifteen or twenty feet down! They're so elegant, they remind me of ballerinas. They'll be zooming along quickly, then effortlessly change direction. At night, you fall asleep to the sound of the rays breaching the surface. The mantas were so plentiful that we became strangely jaded after a while—'Oh, it's just another twenty-foot manta ray. Maybe we'll go look under a rock for a crab!'"

Mantas aren't the only pelagic species of interest around Socorro and neighboring San Benedicto. A variety of sharks are found here with regularity, including white-tips, Galápagos, silkies, silver-tips, and, with less frequency, tiger sharks and whale sharks. (The waters surrounding San Benedicto are featured in Stan Waterman and Howard Hall's *The Man Who Loves Sharks*.) Jacks, wahoo, and giant yellowfin tuna are also regulars here. "I once saw a school of jacks swimming from left to right," Mark said, "and they stretched as far as you could see . . . and they were going by for an hour! At greater depths—one hundred feet or so—you can also come upon schooling hammerheads."

MARK TALKOVIC is an ROV (Remotely Operated Vehicle) pilot for the Monterey Bay Aquarium Research Institute, where he has worked since 1998. He is involved with the daily operations, care, and feeding of the ROV *Ventana*, including the design and fabrication of subsea pressure housings, ROV hardware, tools, and sampling gear. Prior to MBARI, Mark spent eight years as a homeless boat person sailing research vessels (primarily in the Antarctic) and traveling for entertainment. When not at MBARI, he fills his days with occasional contract ROV work, diving, snowboarding, hiking, traveling, and home restoration.

IF YOU GO

➤ **Getting There**: The live-aboards serving Socorro generally depart from Cabo San Lucas (or neighboring San Jose del Cabo), which is served by many major carriers.

➤ **Best Time to Visit**: Socorro charters are led from November through May, when calmer seas make for an easier crossing.

➤ **Accommodations/Guides**: There are several live-aboards that lead expeditions to Socorro, including Solmarv (866-591-4906; www.solmarv.com) and Nautilus Explorer (888-434-8322; www.nautilusexplorer.com).

DESTINATION

31

TRUK LAGOON

RECOMMENDED BY **Cliff Horton**

Countless would-be divers were inspired to take to the sea after watching Jacques Cousteau specials on TV. It was such programming that first started Cliff Horton thinking about Truk Lagoon. "On the specials, I'd heard about how the World War II wrecks in the lagoon had become fabulous reefs," Cliff began. "Much later, I heard that in diving circles it was considered one of the world's top five destinations, but that few people ever got there. It turns out that a friend of mine (who's now a business partner) had been there, and was duly impressed. A few years later I made it as a guest on a boat my friend was captaining at the time. I was amazed at the tremendous amount of marine life on the wrecks—some of them had richer marine life than adjacent natural reefs. Truk is one of the few places where you can experience incredible marine life and incredible history, simultaneously."

Truk Lagoon is situated in the Micronesian state of Chuuk, on the eastern edge of the Caroline Islands, roughly 600 miles southeast of Guam. Most of Chuuk's population resides on the lagoon, which stretches forty miles across. Historically, Chuuk's residents have relied on fishing and farming to exist. Great change came to the region in the early years of World War II, when the Japanese made Truk the stronghold of their South Pacific forces. At times, more than 1,000 ships (patrol boats, mine sweepers, subs, tugs, landing craft, etc.) and 500 aircraft were stationed at Truk, which, with its deep waters, surrounding reef, and ring of mountainous islands, provided a natural fortress. Allied forces made efforts to blockade Truk, and were successful in intercepting supply ships en route. The final blow to the Japanese Empire's Truk garrison was Operation Hailstone, a surprise sweep led by US naval forces in February of 1944. The attack sent seventy ships and hundreds of aircraft to the bottom of Truk Lagoon. It was not until the mid-1960s that Cousteau and other diving pioneers recognized the potential of Truk Lagoon for recreational diving.

OPPOSITE
With seventy sunken Japanese ships, relatively shallow and decidedly calm water, Truk is a wreck diver's paradise.

DESTINATION

32

"I've done wreck diving at other locales," Cliff continued. "Generally, it's been at spots where ships were intentionally sunk to create artificial reefs. The ships were cleaned and stripped accordingly. Or, it's been on natural wrecks that have been exposed to weather and currents that have left the wrecks as piles of metal rather than intact ships. At Truk, the ships have been very well protected by the lagoon. They're not constantly being beaten upon by waves and other ocean action. Since they were sunk while very much in battle, they are full of artifacts. All of these artifacts bring the boats to life. You can really envision a working ship with people doing day-to-day activities. The diving is also fairly easy; most wrecks are at fifty to a hundred feet of depth, there's little current, and the visibility is good. People without a lot of wreck experience can dive safely and comfortably. And the Truk experience is very consistent. The weather varies slightly in terms of how rainy it might be, but the diving experience is very similar, whatever is happening above water."

Everyone who's dived at Truk has a favorite wreck—or five or six! For Cliff Horton, at least three come to mind, with the *Fujikawa Maru* at the top of the list. "The *Fujikawa Maru* was an aircraft ferry, and its role was to deliver aircraft to deployment sites. There's rich marine life around this craft, but what makes it really special is the artifacts that are preserved in its cargo hold, including intact Japanese fighter planes. The cargo hold is very accessible. There's also a well-preserved machine shop with all the equipment you'd expect—lathes, compressor, table, and bandsaws. There are even hand tools still laid out on benches. The *Shinkoku Maru* is another dive I especially like. This ship was an oil tanker, and combines a great amount of sea life with an interesting superstructure. The forward and aft have kingposts and masts that are draped with corals; the deck is covered with soft corals and anemones, and it attracts tons of fish, many small tropical species. There's a pipeline that runs the length of the ship, and anemones grow along the pipe, some four or five feet in diameter. You get great depth variation; the bow is at a depth of about forty-five feet, and the stern is closer to one hundred feet. Inside, there's an operating room (the *Shinkoku Maru* was also used as a medical ship) that includes an autoclave, vials of what once contained medicine, an operating table. There are also several tubs—one for washing, one for soaking, in the Japanese tradition."

Another favorite for Cliff is the *Hoki Maru*. "The *Hoki Maru* is actually half a wreck—the forward portion was destroyed in the bombing," Cliff continued. "It was used to transport equipment and supplies for building airplane runways and roads. There's a cargo hold that's largely intact that's full of heavy machinery, all neatly parked—a bulldozer, water

tankers, steamrollers, tractors, other trucks. You can swim around and look at gauges on the trucks. How well they've been preserved is amazing. (Clients have tried to convince me that some of the trucks were manufactured by Ford—they weren't!)

"There's an interesting phenomenon that occurs at Truk," Cliff offered. "We get many visitors who come because they want to see the wrecks. These are generally men who are curious about WWII or naval history in general. Many times it's a dream trip for a birthday or retirement, and often their wives will come along as good sports, though they have little or no interest in the martial aspects of the trip. After diving Truk with her husband, the wife is so impressed with the marine life, she'll insist that they come back for a second visit. I would never sell anyone on coming to Truk solely for the fish species you'll encounter—you can do a bit better in Indonesia or the Philippines. But Truk's soft corals grow to exceptional sizes—even more so than in Fiji—and our anemones grow like hanging fern baskets."

CLIFF HORTON is an officer and business manger of *Odyssey Adventures* (www.truk odyssey.com), one of Micronesia's premier live-aboard dive boats, located in Truk Lagoon. He is an active recreational scuba instructor and an avid underwater hunter, frequently diving the waters off the coast of northeast Florida, near his home.

IF YOU GO

➤ **Getting There**: Travelers from the western U.S. reach Chuuk via Guam; service is offered by Continental and Continental Micronesia (800-231-0856; www.continental.com).

➤ **Best Time to Visit**: Chuuk has two seasons, according to Cliff—rainy and rainier. January through April there's less rain and greater visibility; in July and August, it's very calm. Divers can visit year round.

➤ **Accommodations**: There are several live-aboards serving Truk, including Odyssey Adventures (800-757-5396; www.trukodyssey.com) and Thorfinn (+69 13-30-3040; www.thorfinn.com). On-shore accommodations include Blue Lagoon Dive Resort (+69 13-30-2727; www.bluelagoondiveresort.com).

➤ **Dive Shops/Guides**: Blue Lagoon Dive Shop (+69 13-30-2796; www.truk-lagoon-dive.com) offers day trips from the Blue Lagoon Dive Resort.

INHAMBANE

RECOMMENDED BY **Sheldon Hey**

Hailing from South Africa, Sheldon Hey has easy access to some superlative diving. But when he decided to seek an adventure, he headed north to Mozambique. "My very first diving experience was in Mozambique, at a place called Ponta d'Ouro," Sheldon began. "This was one of the first places that had opened up to tourism after the conclusion of the country's terrible civil war, and at that time there weren't many visitors, as it was still perceived as rather dangerous—there were still quite a few land mines about. I did my open water certification there, and really fell in love with the place. It was like stepping back in time fifty years. There was very little in the way of infrastructure, but I liked the diving and the taste of the country, rugged and raw undeveloped Africa with a touch of Latin passion.

"A few years later, Mozambique was beginning to get attention as an up-and-coming dive venue. I decided to take a drive-through with a friend who had never been there, and we chose a route that would take us through Maputo [the capital], and on up one-third of the way along the coast. We went ahead with our plan though we'd heard many tales about Mozambique being a terrible place to travel, especially by car. It wasn't the case at all. We especially liked the region around Inhambane town, which rests on a peninsula off the coast. I've been there five times now, and it remains one of my favorite destinations. It's not necessarily for everyone, as there's still a sense of adventure when traveling in Mozambique. I'm always amazed at the energy and lust for life the local people have, considering how little they have in material terms. They love dancing, music, going out. In Inhambane town, you can mix freely with the locals, which adds another dimension to the trip."

The nation of Mozambique lies along the Indian Ocean in southeastern Africa, bordered by South Africa to the south and Tanzania to the north. It boasts 1,500 miles of coastline. Like so many sub-Saharan African nations, Mozambique has had a troubled past.

It was colonized by Portugal after being explored by Vasco da Gama in 1498; the Portuguese were active in the slave trade and invested little in the country and its people. By the mid-1970s, an armed revolution finally broke the Portuguese hold on Mozambique, but shortly after gaining independence, the country erupted in civil war. After more than a million lives were lost, reconciliation was achieved. One of Africa's (and the world's) poorest countries, Mozambique has been making strides toward improving the economic lot of its citizens, though many of its coastal citizens still rely on the sea for their living. The province of Inhambane is in the south of the country, and is considered to be the home of Mozambique's finest diving. Recognizing the tourism potential of Inhambane's unexploited coastline, the government has invested in the region's infrastructure; more accommodations and dive shops are available now than when Sheldon first visited.

"It's fairly simple why the coast of Inhambane stands out as a dive venue," Sheldon continued. "It's perhaps one of the only positive side effects of the civil war. Because the country was brought to its knees, there was very little industrial development. Likewise, there was only subsistence fishing. [Incidentally, greater Inhambane has Mozambique's largest fleet of fishing dhows.] As the seas weren't exploited, very pristine conditions still exist. If you go a few kilometers off the coast, odds are that fishermen have not gotten there. The volumes of fish that you find are unrivaled; likewise, the size. If you're diving in many other spots around the world, the fish you see—grouper or angelfish or what-have-you—are small versions because the mature fish are either caught by fishermen or not given the opportunity to develop. The fish that you can see off Inhambane are the fully grown specimens. You'll come upon brindle bass that are seven feet long and potato bass that are nearly as big, and many manta rays that are in the twenty-foot class." And if you're interested in very big fish, whale sharks are common visitors to the region's waters in the autumn and early winter.

The diving around Inhambane is all land-based; no live-aboards serve the area. However, most of the established dive sites are within a mile or two of shore. "The farthest I've ever gone offshore was about twelve miles," Sheldon added. "The short runs are nice, especially as the sea can get pretty rough in the afternoon. It's all single-level, submerged reef diving. You get down to the bottom where the reef is, and stay there until your time is done. Shallower dives are about forty feet; deeper dives are about a hundred feet. The reef structures are not terrifically impressive. You don't go to Mozambique for the reefs, but for the fish—and for the sense that you're a bit of a pioneer, as relatively few people have been there.

DESTINATION

33

"I remember one dive particularly," Sheldon continued. "My buddy and I went out with a couple who had just opened a dive center, and were as new to the area as we were. In fact, they had just started diving a few weeks before. They wanted to visit a well-regarded site called The Office. They had not been there, but had gotten GPS coordinates from one of the other resorts. We went offshore about twelve miles, and dropped in. On this day, we could see all the way to the bottom (about one hundred feet) where sharks were cruising. When we got to bottom, a huge potato bass came out of the gloom. Usually they're quite shy, but this specimen was very curious—it was as if he wanted to learn more about this strange creature who was blowing bubbles. As I was being observed by the potato bass, my buddy made a noise. I turned, and about seven feet in front of me was a twenty-foot manta ray. I almost dropped my regulator as the animal seemed to flip over the top of me so it wouldn't hit me. It was so large, yet so silent. You get a real fright seeing something that large get so close so silently. Toward the end, a bull shark—which I'd never seen before—came circling into the periphery. It was a pretty memorable dive, considering we had no idea where to go."

SHELDON HEY is the general manager of Dive the World (www.dive-the-world.com), a travel agency specializing in diving travel around the world. A PADI Master Scuba Diver Trainer, he's traveled to Africa, Southeast Asia, and the South Pacific on diving adventures.

IF YOU GO

➤ **Getting There**: Inhambane Province is served by Pelican Air (+27 11-973-3649; www.pelicanair.co.za) via Johannesburg, South Africa. Johannesburg is served by South African Airways (27 11-978-5313; www.flysaa.com), United (800-864-8331; www.united.com), and Delta (800-221-1212; www.delta.com).

➤ **Best Time to Visit**: Diving is good year round, though February and August can be very windy. The best time for whale sharks is October through March.

➤ **Accommodations**: Sheldon recommends Hotel Marinhos (+25 82 32 9015; hotel marinhos@ananzi.co.za) in Tofo, and Guinjata Resort (+27 13-741-2795; www.guinjata.com) for more of a resort experience.

➤ **Dive Shops/Guides**: Diversity Scuba (+25 82-32-9002; www.diversityscuba.com) leads day trips from Tofo.

MERGUI ARCHIPELAGO

RECOMMENDED BY **Ingo Siewert**

Thailand—specifically the west coast of Thailand and the Andaman Sea—is a recognized dive destination. Scuba enthusiasts are quite familiar with the lures of the Similan Islands and Richelieu Rock, among other venues. The waters of the Andaman Sea off peninsular Thailand's northwestern neighbor Myanmar (formerly known as Burma) offer many of the same attractions, with one difference. "Put simply, Myanmar is not overrun with visitors," Ingo Siewert began. "I love the Similans, but at many of the sites there you might be moored with ten other boats. In Myanmar, you have the same quality of diving, and you usually have places to yourself. For live-aboards departing from greater Phuket, a place like the Mergui Archipelago is quite easy to reach. Overall, I think it's a better dive value."

The Mergui Archipelago consists of some 800 islands off the southern coast of Myanmar, stretching north from the Thai border nearly 200 miles and encompassing over 14,000 square miles of marine territory—much of it unexplored. The islands—blanketed with a mix of rainforest, mangroves, and white sand beaches—are largely untouched by the imprint of humankind. This is due in part to the island's isolation from both Thai and Myanmar population centers, and in part to politics. After gaining independence from Great Britain in 1948, (then) Burma closed its doors (and waters) to outsiders. Fast-forward nearly fifty years. Recognizing the potential of an area called the Burma Banks (a series of sea mounts roughly one hundred miles northwest of the Similans, well regarded for shark encounters)—and perhaps anticipating the potential for crowding in Thai waters as more Westerners discovered their appeals—several Phuket dive operators began negotiations with the Myanmar government. Initially, they hoped to gain access just to the banks. Their first forays found little success, but in 1997 visitors were permitted (for a fee) to visit not only Burma Banks, but the inshore areas of the Mergui Archipelago.

DESTINATION

34

The underwater environs around Mergui Archipelago are every bit as interesting as the terrain above. There are inland reefs that offer incredible species diversity; offshore reefs that offer better visibility and more robust coral; and pinnacles, which have the potential to attract large pelagics. Divers seeking everchanging underwater topography will not be disappointed here! One promise the waters of the Mergui may not always be able to deliver on is big animals. "When I first started traveling up to Myanmar, many people went in hopes of seeing sharks," Ingo continued. "While there's always a good chance of seeing mantas, reef sharks, even whale sharks, the smaller fish and invertebrate life are much more prevalent. This—and the sense of adventure that's still very real here—are the main reasons to visit Mergui. I encourage visitors to embrace the diversity of marine life, whether it be reef fish or macro creatures. The macro life is amazing in these parts." (This being said, some nine species of shark have been recorded around Mergui, including bull, tiger, hammerhead, gray reef, nurse, mako, and spinner sharks.)

It's likely to be some years before all the possibilities of Mergui are mapped out by dive operators. Nonetheless, in the ten years that the archipelago has been explored, a number of superlative sites have been identified. Fan Forest Pinnacle, near the Thai border, is blanketed—as its name might imply—with sea fans, exceptional for their size and vibrant orange hue. The pinnacle rises from tremendous depths, so the potential for spotting large pelagics is good. Another celebrated site is Shark Cave (sometimes called Three Islets), which is a bit farther north near Great Swinton Island. The cave in question is home to nurse sharks, and gray reef sharks (and more rarely, white-tip reef sharks) are sometimes encountered in the tunnel leading into the cave. Though sharks gave this venue its name, visitors who take the time may remember it more for the macro life present on the surrounding reefs. Harlequin ghost pipefish, tigertail sea horses, mantis shrimp, and cuttlefish are regularly witnessed here; there are also brilliantly colored anemones.

Black Rock, perhaps the most celebrated of Mergui sites, lies farther to the north, toward the center of the archipelago. A complex mix of currents make the dives here challenging, but it's worth the effort. Black Rock affords Mergui visitors the best opportunity for encounters with larger rays and sharks. "On one dive at Black Rock," Ingo recalled, "we came upon a whale shark cruising among a group of mantas. I wanted to tell the other divers that we may as well leave, because it wasn't going to get any better than that. Then the next day, we had a dozen manta rays around us in a very concentrated space!" Mobula and eagle rays, white-tip, silver-tip, and black-tip sharks are also seen here. Even at Black Rock,

OPPOSITE
Lucky visitors to the Mergui Archipelago will encounter the Moken people, or Sea Gypsies, who live much of the year in their boats.

DESTINATION

34

one must remember the Mergui mantra: Don't forget the small stuff! Black-spotted puffer-fish, spotted hawkfish, scorpion fish, and blue-ringed angelfish are regulars here.

When he was leading divers around the Mergui Archipelago, Ingo enjoyed exploring the islands above water. "The bird life is very rich on these islands, and worth experienc-ing," he said. "If the group I was leading was laid-back and didn't want to dive every available opportunity, we might do some canoeing in the mangroves. The islands are almost com-pletely uninhabited, though on occasion we might run into the Sea Gypsies." The Myanmar Sea Gypsies, also known as Salons, are members of the Moken ethnic group of Myanmar and Thailand, and sustain themselves hunting and gathering the riches of the sea. "The Sea Gypsies live on longtail boats with thatched roofs, much like they did 300 years ago," Ingo added.

There's one other bonus to diving in the Mergui Archipelago—to get back to Phuket, you have to motor in close proximity to Richelieu Rock, the Similans, and many of the other signature spots of Thai scuba. If you allow enough time on your Andaman adventure, you can enjoy both.

INGO SIEWERT works with Dive the World (www.dive-the-world.com) as a member of the sales team. He has been diving the Asia Pacific region for many years, and served as a dive-master and cruise director on live-aboard boats in Myanmar, Thailand, and Indonesia since 1999. Ingo lives in Phuket, Thailand, with his wife and two children.

▰▰ IF YOU GO ▰▰

➤ **Getting There**: The live-aboards that serve the Mergui Archipelago generally depart from Phuket, Khao Lak, or Ranong (the latter two towns north of Phuket). The island of Phuket can be reached via Bangkok on a number of international carriers, including Japan, Malaysia, Northwest, and United Airlines.

➤ **Best Time to Visit**: The diving season in Myanmar is October to May, with the latter part of the season yielding the most manta and whale shark sightings.

➤ **Accommodations**: Ingo recommends the live-aboards MV *Sai Mai* and MV *Faah Yai*. Dive the World (+66 83-505-7794; www.dive-the-world.com) highlights these and other live-aboard options.

BONAIRE

RECOMMENDED BY **Dee Scarr**

The license plate for the island of Bonaire bears the slogan "Divers Paradise." That this slogan is written in English is somewhat curious, as Bonaire is part of the Kingdom of the Netherlands. But considering the great care Bonaireans have taken in protecting their reefs and waters—and that much of the diving is done here from the shore, with divers driving from spot to spot in a rented Jeep or car—it makes perfectly good sense.

"I'd been working in the Bahamas for several years when a client mentioned that I would love Bonaire and its shore diving," Dee Scarr began. "I talked to Peter Hughes at one of the dive trade shows, and soon after ended up coming to work at Bonaire. I never left. For me, Bonaire means gentle diving and very healthy reefs. A visit to another island a few years back put Bonaire in perspective. I was enjoying my dive, thinking it was a nice spot, when I thought I saw someone coming out of the water with a spear gun. I asked the divemaster about it, and he said, 'Oh yeah. They can use spear guns here.' It was a shock for me, and a reality check. The presence of spear fishing changes the behavior of fish, as you might imagine. Spear fishing was banned at Bonaire in 1971. The island has been extremely progressive on many other conservation measures. I haven't dived anywhere else for ten years."

Though situated just fifty miles north of Venezuela at the southern end of the Caribbean, the island of Bonaire is at first more reminiscent of the American southwest than a tropical idyll—this thanks to a climate that's atypically arid for this part of the world. Initially settled by the Caiquetios people from Venezuela, Bonaire's first European discoverers were led by the Spaniard Amerigo Vespucci in 1499. By the early 1600s, the Dutch had captured the island from Spain, and have continued to hold Bonaire (along with Aruba and Curaçao) as part of the Lesser (or Netherlands) Antilles. Above water, Bonaire is home to an odd array of animals. Wild donkeys and goats roam the cactus-studded island, descendants

of long-ago domestic stock, along with iguanas and a sizable flock of flamingos. Below, it's home to some of the Caribbean's most intact and healthy reefs—"the Caribbean as it used to be," as Bonaire dive-travel brochures like to proclaim. This thanks to conservation measures alluded to above—which included early protection of turtle eggs and nests (1961), banning of coral collection (1975), and the establishment of the Bonaire Marine Park (1979), which extends all the way around the island, as well as around neighboring Klein Bonaire. Thanks to the lack of runoff (due to a lack of rain), visibility is excellent around Bonaire, averaging over one hundred feet, and sometimes approaching 150 feet.

OPPOSITE
Thanks to aggressive conservation efforts, Bonaire boasts some of the Caribbean's healthiest reef systems.

"The thing that makes Bonaire so special, and such an excellent shore-diving locale, is that the whole island is surrounded by a lush, living coral reef," Dee continued. "It's anywhere from a two-minute to a five-minute swim from the beach. The reefs shelve off gently to about thirty feet. What I learned at Bonaire is that reefs can be more beautiful if they aren't sheer drop-offs, as the coral and sponges get more light and become more vibrant. At thirty feet, there's a more pronounced drop-off. On the shelves and the drop-off, there's a wonderful assortment of reef fish, though not many bigger animals. In places, you'll find tarpon to three or four feet long; on night dives, they'll hunt by your light. But at Bonaire, you don't go out hoping to find any species in particular; you dive to appreciate the overall picture."

Dee Scarr has long believed that people can forge a closer connection with underwater creatures if they're able to physically come in contact with them. "Nothing can touch you emotionally if you can't literally touch it," she said. "With Touch the Sea, I take what I've learned over my diving career and apply it to help people feel more comfortable touching sea creatures in a respectful, nonobtrusive way. One of the animals I look for is the scorpion fish, which, because of their good defense mechanisms, can be very comfortable around respectful divers. If a diver has good buoyancy control and the fish are not agitated, it's possible to interact with them. I also like to find sharptail eels. They are also very self-confident, thanks to their defense mechanism—a layer of distasteful mucous that puts off most predators. Of course, this defense mechanism doesn't affect divers, so these eels are often very comfortable with us, allowing us to gently stroke them.

"There was an occasion a few years back when I was doing a little dive on a stretch of reef just outside Kralendijik. Technically it was the harbor, but hardly anyone dives there. As I was diving, a fish trap came down. (Small-scale fish traps are allowed in the reserve.) I surfaced, hoping I'd be able to get the fisherman to move the trap and was delighted when I saw it was someone I knew—an older fellow named Francis. When I asked if he would mind

DESTINATION

35

moving it, he said, 'Dee, I didn't know this was *your* reef. I'd be happy to move down!' He then pulled his trap up, rowed his boat 200 yards down the reef, and set it again."

DEE SCARR is a PADI scuba and specialty instructor, an experienced naturalist, and author of three books: *Touch the Sea*, *Coral's Reef*, and *The Gentle Sea*. Her articles and photos appear in *The New Guide to the Bonaire Marine Park*, *Dive Training*, *Skin Diver*, and other publications. She leads trips to select sites around Bonaire through her company, Touch the Sea (www.touchthesea.com), with the goal of helping guests better understand marine creatures. She has received many honors, including Beneath the Sea's Diver of the Year award for environment, the Boston Sea Rovers' Diver of the Year award, and the PADI-SeaSpace Environmental Awareness award. Dee is very active with the Action on Behalf of Coral project, which has the goal of educating divers on how to distinguish live coral, recognize its fragility, and understand its importance to the ecosystem. Dee was inducted into the Women Divers Hall of Fame in 2000.

IF YOU GO

➤ **Getting There**: Bonaire is served from the U.S. with direct flights from Atlanta on Delta (800-221-1212; www.delta.com); and from Newark and Houston on Continental (800-231-0856; www.continental.com).

➤ **Best Time to Visit**: Diving is good throughout the year.

➤ **Accommodations**: Captain Don's Habitat (800-327-6709; www.habitatdiveresorts.com) has been hosting divers for many years. A wide range of other lodgings options are listed at www.infobonaire.com.

➤ **Dive Shops/Guides**: Dee Scarr leads divers through her company, Touch the Sea (www.touchthesea.com). A number of other dive-shop operators are listed at www.info bonaire.com.

DESTINATION

35

DOUBTFUL SOUND

RECOMMENDED BY **Amy West**

The saltwater attractions of Doubtful Sound and Fiordland are a direct result of a freshwater phenomenon germane to the southwestern coast of the South Island of New Zealand, as Amy West explained. "Parts of Fiordland get as much as twenty-five feet of rain each year," she began. "This rain runs off the mountains that border the coast, taking with it tannins from the soil. The dark brown fresh water layers on top of the saltwater of the fjords; over thirty feet of freshwater can accumulate on top of the salt water. As a result, next to no light permeates the salt water, which is in itself very clear. This gives a variety of sea life—especially invertebrates—the impression that the creatures are residing in water that's hundreds or thousands of feet in depth, when in fact they could be in water that's only forty or fifty feet deep. As a result, you can encounter some extreme deep-water species without imploding or buying a submarine. Around the Fiordlands, it only takes twenty or thirty seconds to reach the deep-sea world."

Fiordland is a 4,600-square-mile national park along the very southwestern coast of the South Island of New Zealand, bordering the Tasman Sea. Here, the southern reach of the rugged Southern Alps, some approaching 9,000 feet, butt against the coast, and jagged fjords cut in among the mountains. The combination of steep mountains, dark green forest, snow-capped peaks, foaming waterfalls, and fingers of blue fjords make Fiordland one of the most visually stunning temperate regions in the world. (This has been recognized by UNESCO, which named the park a World Heritage Site as Te Moana O Atawhenua.) There are fifteen fjords in all, with Milford and Doubtful Sound being the best known. Fiordland has long attracted hearty adventurers, most notably trekkers; after all, it's home to what many consider to be the world's most beautiful hike, the Milford Track. This hike ends at Milford Sound, the most popular diving site in the region.

In the veritable naturalist's wonderland that is Fiordland, Doubtful Sound stands out as something special. It took its name from Captain James Cook, who felt it was "doubtful" whether the sound could be navigated by his sailing craft. Doubtful Sound has three distinct arms, with the Deep Cove arm reaching twenty-five miles from its eastern point to the open sea. It reaches over 1,300 feet in depth in places, and has two waterfalls (Helena and Browne Falls) that cascade 2,000 feet. Above the surface of the sound, visitors will find New Zealand fur seals and Fiordland crested penguins. Below, much of the animal life of interest to divers is considerably less ambulatory.

"When I moved to Dunedin, New Zealand, I was looking for short-term work until a research job at the university started," Amy continued. "As part of another project, they were looking for help counting black coral, which became my role. Not knowing a great deal about it, I thought the black coral would be black. Instead, it's white when viewed alive in its habitat." The living tissue of black coral, in fact, can take on many vivid colors. The name is derived from the coral's exoskeleton, which is dark brown or black. Black coral has a tree-like structure, and is popular for use in jewelry. Despite its predilection for great depths, it is considered endangered, as in some places divers will go to depths of 250 feet to harvest it. "There are eight or nine other species that are generally found in very deep water that can be seen in relatively shallow water around Fiordland," Amy continued. These include brachiopods, stony corals, red corals, sea pens, wavy-lined perch, glass sponges, and snake stars."

Part of the thrill of diving Doubtful Sound is getting to Doubtful Sound. While the head of the fjord at Milford can be reached by road, Doubtful Sound can only be reached by boat (via Milford) or over land. "To get there, we drove to Te Anau, loaded up a Zodiac with our gear, then crossed Lake Te Anau, loaded a Hilux truck, and then drove over a significant pass before dropping down to the fjord. I was blown away by the scenery and how tall the mountains are; it's almost as steep below the surface. Entering the water is an odd experience. When you're in the dark fresh water, it's disorienting; you feel like you're drunk or have vertigo. Then you pop out into the salt water, which has excellent visibility, and is usually warmer. In Fiordland, you can be in three distinctly different elements in twenty seconds—on the surface looking at 6,000-foot mountains, in the dark of the fresh water, and then the clear of the salt water."

If you book a trip to Doubtful Sound, your dive operator will likely take you to Te Awaatu Channel Marine Reserve—popularly referred to as The Gut. The 230-acre reserve rests near the mouth of the fjord, between Secretary Island and Bauza Island, and is shallow

OPPOSITE
An abundance of freshwater feeds into Doubtful Sound, creating unique conditions that bring deep water creatures into much shallower water.

DESTINATION

36

enough for divers to access the region's celebrated red and black corals. "There are resident bottlenose dolphins in Doubtful Sound—very large by U.S. standards," Amy added. "They can be observed around The Gut."

AMY WEST realized at an early age that she wanted to be a marine biologist, even though she hailed from Durango, Colorado. She graduated from the University of the Virgin Islands with a marine biology degree. After serving in the Peace Corps in Gabon for a fisheries project, she obtained a master's degree in marine science in New Zealand, where her research involved exploration of a remote fjord with a manned submersible to document life beyond scuba depths. An internship at MBARI led her back to the United States after being abroad for ten years. Her work has since taken her to Antarctica, the Bering Sea, and all around Monterey Bay aboard a sailing educational vessel. Amy fosters her love for ocean mysteries through creative writing; she's currently working on a young-adult novel focused on deep-sea adventures and deep-ocean conservation.

IF YOU GO

➤ **Getting There**: Air New Zealand (800-262-1234; www.airnewzealand.com) offers service to Te Anau via Queenstown through Air New Zealand Link. North American travelers will reach Queenstown via Auckland or Christchurch.

➤ **Best Time to Visit**: Diving is done year round. It rains nearly twenty-five feet a year, so there's no dry season you can count on.

➤ **Accommodations**: Te Anau and Manapouri are the main visitor hubs for Fiordland, and the Fiordland Website (www.fiordland.org.nz) lists a range of accommodations.

➤ **Dive Shops/Guides**: Several outfitters lead day and/or overnight diving trips to Milford and Doubtful Sounds, including Fiordland Expeditions (+64 3-249-9005; www.fiordlandexpeditions.co.nz) and Tawaki Dive & Scenic Tours (+64 3-212-7757; www.tawakidive.co.nz).

POOR KNIGHTS ISLANDS

RECOMMENDED BY **Matthew Oldfield**

New Zealand's Poor Knights Islands are said to take their name from a French toastlike pudding that they somehow resembled in the eyes of Captain James Cook, the first European explorer to visit here. For latter-day English explorer Matthew Oldfield, Poor Knights proved a feast. "I first learned about Poor Knights from a few of my Scubazoo colleagues, who had gone down from Malaysia to film killer whales, which come into the islands each year to feed on mating stingrays. When we were commissioned to create our coffee-table book *Reef*, we wanted to expand beyond tropical climes to include cooler waters, and Poor Knights was included. After spending nine days there, I felt it was the kind of place I could relocate to—and that's saying something, as we work from near Sipadan!"

Poor Knights Islands lie roughly twelve miles east of the Tutukaka coast, in the Northland region of the North Island of New Zealand. The two predominant islands of the chain are Aorangi and Tawhiti Rahi, with several smaller islands in between. Volcanic in origin, the islands of the Poor Knights chain have steep cliffs and steep drop-offs, in some places more than 300 feet not far off shore. Aorangi and Tawhiti Rahi were once occupied by a band of Maori, but in the early 1800s, much of the tribe was massacred by members of the Hikutu tribe from the mainland. Thereafter, remaining members of the Poor Knights Maori band declared the islands *tapu* (meaning sacred/forbidden, and off limits), and the islands have been uninhabited ever since. Today the islands and surrounding water are part of a marine reserve—and are considered one of the North Island's premier scuba sites.

Two qualities conspire to make Poor Knights special—the proximity of the East Auckland current, and the archipelago's volcanic origins. "At Poor Knights, you get a great mix of species," Matthew continued, "as you have a mix of warm and temperate waters.

Temperatures can vary by ten to fifteen degrees, depending on where you're diving. The warm current brings in many tropical species that aren't generally found around New Zealand. The topography is stunning, dotted with caves and undersea arches. This makes for some stunning photographic settings. With the open Pacific to the east, you never know what might swim by, and this introduces an element of uncertainty and excitement."

There are scores of dive sites scattered around the islands; most are within a few minutes' run of each other, with the exception of those at the Pinnacles, which lie five miles south of the main islands. Of these, none is more celebrated than Blue Mao Mao Arch. "Blue Mao Mao Arch is the archetypal dive at Poor Knights, and presents what is perhaps one of the archetypal dive images to be found anywhere," Matthew continued. "It's one of the biggest arches at Poor Knights, some sixty-five feet across, and there are two holes in the top that let in shafts of sunlight. It's quite like a cathedral. Within the arch are vast schools of blue mao mao, a veritable fish soup. These fish are electric blue, and they barely seem to move. I just sat on the bottom and stared up, utterly captivated." Moray eels—both yellow and gray—are also often found in the arch.

Another "must-dive" spot at Poor Knights is Riko Riko Cave, reputed to be the world's largest sea cave, quite capable of accommodating a sailing yacht. "When I was there, we had a killer whale come into the cave," Matthew said. "But it was also wonderful for smaller animal life, which is my primary interest. I saw some wonderful nudibranchs there and at Poor Knights in general. I also came upon lovely triplefin blennies—bright pink with purple candy stripes." Thanks to its popularity among boaters as well as divers, you'll tend to find company at Riko Riko, though that shouldn't dissuade you from visiting; with a mix of shallow and deeper water, Riko Riko is ideal for groups that combine beginners and more seasoned divers.

The Pinnacles, and nearby Sugarloaf, an isolated rock stack, were another attraction for Matthew. "Sugarloaf is very exposed to the open ocean," he continued. "On the dive, you drop into a big gully. At times it becomes filled with huge bull rays, cruising back and forth. My coworkers tell me that many of the arches and caves around Poor Knights will get congregations of rays like this, stacks of a hundred or 150 at a time, and that it's quite an experience to get underneath them and look up. I didn't experience the rays in this abundance; a few weeks before my visit, the killer whales had been in munching on them, tossing around these three-to-six-foot-wide stingrays like they were Frisbees."

OPPOSITE
A manta soars gracefully through one of the many arches that dot the subsurface terrain of Poor Knights Islands.

DESTINATION

37

MATTHEW OLDFIELD is a photographer with Scubazoo (www.scubazoo.com), a team of professional underwater cameramen and photographers who have an intense love for and appreciation of the marine world. He started diving in 1990 in preparation for an expedition to Belize, researching the behavior of moray eels and squirrelfish, and has since logged more than 3,000 dives at locations in Southeast Asia, Central America, and the UK. Matthew holds a biology degree from Worcester College, Oxford University, and is a PADI divemaster with TDI Advanced Nitrox, Extended Range, and Rebreather qualifications. After working in the stock photography business as a picture researcher, he left London to spend a year as a divemaster on Sipadan, Malaysia, and soon joined Scubazoo. Matthew now manages the publications side of Scubazoo, developing the huge image library as well as shooting and writing for a variety of magazines and publishing companies. His photos and writing appear in Scubazoo's coffee-table books *Sipadan, Mabul, Kapalai*, and *Reef*. Matthew has also become a valuable member of Scubazoo's broadcast filming team having worked on the first *UK Survivor* show in 2001 and more recently, Channel 5's "Killer Shark Live."

IF YOU GO

➤ **Getting There**: Whangarei is served by Air New Zealand (800-262-1234; www.air newzealand.com) via Auckland.

➤ **Best Time to Visit**: Poor Knights can be dived year round, though October through March is considered the best time.

➤ **Accommodations**: Destination Northland (+64 9-402-7683; www.northlandnz.com) has a comprehensive list of lodgings options in and around Whangarei, the region's tourism hub.

➤ **Dive Shops/Guides**: A number of operators serve the Poor Knights Islands, including Dive Tutukaka (+64 9-434-3867; www.diving.co.nz). Poor Knights Liveaboards (www.dive poorknights.com) is one of several live-aboard options in the region.

CAPE HATTERAS

RECOMMENDED BY **Dave Sommers**

"Wreck diving drew me in through its connection to history," Dave Sommers began. "When you can add in an abundance of sea life, it's hard to beat. Cape Hatteras gives you both—plus a great diversity of species. We get marine life that comes south from the North Atlantic with the Labrador Current, and Caribbean species that are brought north with the Gulf Stream. All of this tremendous sea life gathers around the wrecks. You never know what you're going to find off Cape Hatteras, and I guess that's why it continues to hold my attention."

Cape Hatteras is part of the barrier islands that make up the Outer Banks. It's the most eastern point in the state of North Carolina—and for that matter, the most eastern point below the Mason-Dixon Line. The confluence of the Labrador and Gulf Stream currents off Cape Hatteras has over time created an obstacle called Diamond Shoals, which reaches some miles to sea. The shallowness of the shoals, combined with the frequency and fury of storms that lash the coast hereabouts, have made Cape Hatteras the site of countless ship-wrecks. The first recorded wreck was in 1585, a ship called the *Tyger*, part of England's second expedition to North America. Perhaps the most famous was the USS *Monitor*, one of the US Navy's first ironclad warships. The *Monitor* engaged the USS *Merrimack* (renamed the *Virginia* by the Confederates) in March of 1862 in Hampton Roads, and the battle was considered a draw, though a victory for the concept of ironclad ships. It foundered near the Diamond Shoals in December of that year in a storm. (Storms and shoals weren't the only hazards facing ships plying the Gulf Stream off Hatteras; German U-boats claimed a number of ships during both world wars.)

There are scores of wrecks off Cape Hatteras that dive-charter operators frequent; in-shore, there are a host of artificial reef/wrecks that are of less interest to seasoned divers.

DESTINATION

38

When pressed to name a favorite, Dave was quick to reply: "The one I'm on today! Each one has its own special flavor. Some are fascinating junk piles, some have consistently good visibility. Others almost always have great fish life. Two wrecks that are among the most popular are the *Proteus* and the *Tarpon*." The *Proteus* was a passenger freighter that sunk in 1918 while attempting to round the cape without running lights to avoid German subs; it collided with a tanker, the *Cushing*. The site of the *Proteus* generally offers clear water, and is an excellent spot to find sharks, sea turtles, and occasionally mantas. "People who come out to dive want to see sharks," Dave continued, "and I can almost guarantee that experience around a wreck like the *Proteus*—especially sand tigers. I've been in the water with 200 or 300 at a time." Sand tigers—also known as ragged-tooth sharks—have an impressive array of teeth and menacing yellow eyes, making for a perfect picture of shark malice, though in the waters off Cape Hatteras they are not considered dangerous.

The *Tarpon* was a US Navy submarine that had served in the Pacific theater in World War II. It had a somewhat ignominious end in 1956, when it sunk off the cape as it was being towed to a scrap yard. The *Tarpon* rests at nearly 150 feet, but those able to make the dive will be able to access the control room and torpedo hatches. "The *Tarpon* is a great spot to find lionfish," Dave continued. "And you never know what pelagics might show up—that goes for the *Tarpon*, and many of the other wrecks. I've encountered nurse sharks, lemon sharks, tiger sharks, oceanic white-tip, silkies, makos, and bull sharks; four kinds of rays; three species of tuna; loggerhead and leatherback turtles; in short, everything from tropical blennies to goliath groupers. We've had pilot whales, and even whale sharks. Visitors should know that most of the diving is pretty advanced, using anchor lines. There's a strong current, a lot of deeper dives, and often rough seas. It's a little wild out there, but perhaps because of that, there's less people pressure."

Toward the end of the 2007 season, Dave and his wife had an experience that encapsulates the best of wreck diving, and the best of what Cape Hatteras has to offer. "My wife and I were diving out on the *Kassandra* [the *Kassandra Louloudis*, a Greek freighter that was torpedoed by a German sub in March of 1942 as it came to the aid of a torpedoed American oil tanker, the *Acme*]," Dave recounted. "We had seen some dishware in the sand, and we were digging the dishes out. Suddenly it became very dark. At first we couldn't tell why, and then we realized it was a massive animal body blocking the light. I thought it was a large shark, but then the animal turned and came toward us—it was a manta ray. It stopped an arm's length away and looked at us. We were so close, we could see the eye rotating. It then slowly

OPPOSITE
The remains of the
MS Aeolus, *a*
cable repair ship,
make up one of a
number of naval
wrecks off of Cape
Hatteras.

DESTINATION

38

hovered up, like a spaceship, and went out of sight. We gathered up the dishes we'd found and put them in our goody bag, and struck out after the manta . . . and sure enough, we found it again before it was time to surface."

DAVE SOMMERS operates Dive Hatteras with his wife, Ann; together, they have more than forty years diving experience. For several years he had a wreck-diving operation out of Ocean City, Maryland, but after just one season at Cape Hatteras, he moved the operation there for good.

IF YOU GO

➤ **Getting There**: The closest major airport to Cape Hatteras is in Norfolk, Virginia, which is roughly three and a half hours away; Norfolk is served by many major carriers.

➤ **Best Time to Visit**: The diving season is May to October. Visibility can vary depending on ocean conditions.

➤ **Accommodations**: Hatteras City and Buxton are the main points of departure for Cape Hatteras diving expeditions. The Dive Hatteras Website has an extensive list of accommodations at www.divehatteras.com/areainfo.htm.

➤ **Dive Shops/Guides**: There are a number of charter outfits serving Hatteras wreck-diving enthusiasts, including Dive Hatteras (703-818-1850; www.divehatteras.com) and Outer Banks Diving (252-986-1056; www.outerbanksdiving.com).

DESTINATION

38

FATHOM FIVE NATIONAL PARK

RECOMMENDED BY **Dan Orr**

"The year was 1976, and Canadian pop-music star Gordon Lightfoot had recently released his song 'The Wreck of the *Edmund Fitzgerald*,'" Dan Orr began. "We listened to the song again and again as we drove north through the night from Ohio toward Tobermory, Ontario, site of Fathom Five National Marine Park. It only increased our anticipation—after all, we were heading to Tobermory to dive the *Arabia* and the other wrecks around Fathom Five." (For those unfamiliar with the tune, Lightfoot's song recounts the 1975 sinking of the *Edmund Fitzgerald*, a freighter carrying iron ore, in Lake Superior; the lives of twenty-nine crewmen were lost.)

Fathom Five National Marine Park comprises forty-five square miles of Lake Huron (the middle lake of the Great Lakes) off the tip of the Bruce Peninsula, which juts out into the lake to help create Georgian Bay to the east. The strata of the region is considered the northern reach of the Niagara Escarpment, a series of dolomite rock formations that stretch from its southern terminus at Niagara Falls. Geologists estimate that the Niagara Escarpment dates back 400 million years, to a time when the Great Lakes were a shallow, tropical sea. Around Tobermory and adjoining Bruce Peninsula National Park, the Niagara Escarpment is marked by rugged cliffs on its eastern edge along Georgian Bay and sandy shallows along its western flank, Lake Huron.

The waters off Tobermory are regarded as the epicenter of Canadian (and perhaps Great Lakes) wreck diving, a treasure trove for those interested in maritime history and archaeology. Beginning in the 1850s, there was a significant increase in shipping traffic in the region; schooners headed north to deliver supplies to budding lumber towns along Georgian Bay, and returned to points south hauling lumber to help build out the Midwest. (By the 1890s, schooners were increasingly displaced by steamships.) During the frequent storms that are visited upon Lake Huron, ships in the vicinity of Tobermory would seek refuge in the two sheltered harbors—Big Tub and Little Tub—near the town. Many did not make it. Today, Big Tub and Little Tub harbors are home to five wrecks, and Fathom Five boasts twenty-two. "Tobermory is named for a town on the Isle of Mull in Scotland," Dan continued, "and it's not unlike being in Scotland—that is, it's cool, often misty, and the people are exceedingly friendly. Put another way—it's the kind of place where you'd expect to see a nineteenth-century shipwreck!"

Tobermory and Fathom Five have wrecks for divers of all levels. "There are many ways to experience the wrecks," Dan explained. "Many are very close to shore, and people can dive from the shoreline. There are some tugs in Little Tug Harbor that rest in just fifteen to twenty feet of water. One fascinating ship in Big Tub Harbor is the *Sweepstakes*, a schooner built in 1867. It was stranded outside the harbor at Cove Island, and sunk as salvagers tried to drift it back into the harbor. Though it's been on the bottom since 1885, the hull is virtually intact, thanks in part to assistance from the local diving community. It's in such shallow water that you can stand on the railing and have your head on the surface. This and the tugs are a great introduction to wreck diving."

The wreck that has most imprinted itself upon Dan Orr's memory is the *Arabia*, a 131-foot barque (a sailing ship with fore and aft sails on the stern mast and square sails on the other masts) built in 1853 that came to rest in 1884 in 105 feet of water off Tobermory near Echo Island. (Oddly enough, the *Arabia* almost came to rest near Tobermory in 1883 around Flowerpot Island, where she ran aground. She was refloated, repaired, and returned to service for one more year.) "After my first trip there in 1976, the *Arabia* became a focal point of the underwater archaeology section of an advanced diving course I'd developed at Wright State University in the late seventies," Dan said. "As part of the course, we created a simulation of the *Arabia* at the bottom of a local quarry, visited nautical museums, then dove progressively deeper wrecks, building toward the trip to Tobermory."

Discovered in 1971, the *Arabia* holds great appeal for wreck enthusiasts, as it's a rare example of a nearly intact nineteenth-century wooden sailing ship, in a place where waters are clear enough to take it in in all its wonder. The ship rests upright. Much of the hull is intact, as is the ship's impressive bow, with several anchors in place, as if ready to drop. The ship's wheel is preserved, attached to some decking that rests off the starboard side of the stern quarter. Great Lakes dive enthusiasts also point to another less obvious benefit to the *Arabia*—it's yet to be infested with zebra mussels. It's not a dive for beginners; the

DESTINATION

39

water is cold and currents can be strong. (An irony pointed out by writer Glenn Garnett is that while no crewmen perished when the *Arabia* went down, more than a dozen divers have died while investigating its secrets.) But most agree it's a dive that's worth the time it takes to gain the know-how necessary to experience it.

"This is one of those unique diving experiences that fills a special place in your heart that's shared with the other few treasured experiences of your life!" Dan enthused. "I was so taken with the *Arabia* and Tobermory that I asked my wife to marry me there (above water). On the hundredth anniversary of the sinking of the *Arabia*, I led a dive team from Wright State to Tobermory to commemorate the event," Dan added. "We made one dive to place an inscribed granite memorial stone next to the wreck site, which reads 'Celebrate the history and the experience.'"

DAN ORR has been involved in virtually all aspects of the diving industry for more than forty years. In 2005, he was named president/CEO of Divers Alert Network (DAN) after having been executive vice president and chief operating officer for more than ten years. In 1991, Orr was named DAN director of training responsible for developing and implementing DAN training programs, including the internationally successful DAN Oxygen First Aid Course. Prior to coming to DAN, Orr was the associate diving safety officer at Florida State University and director of diver training programs at Wright State University in Dayton, Ohio. Orr has a bachelor's and master's degree in biology and has authored and contributed to many books and magazine articles, including as co-author of *Scuba Diving Safety* (2007) and DAN's *Pocket Guide for Diving Safety* series. Orr has been a featured speaker at Our World-Underwater, Underwater Canada, Boston Sea Rovers, International Conference on Underwater Education, SeaSpace, Undersea and Hyperbaric Medical Society (UHMS), as well as many others. He has also been the recipient of many awards for diving safety, including the Leonard Greenstone Award for Diving Safety, the NOGI from the Academy of Underwater Arts & Sciences in Sports/Education, the Our World-Underwater Award, Beneath the Sea's Diver of the Year in Education, and Associate Boston Sea Rover. Orr currently serves on the boards of directors of organizations such as Diving Equipment and Marketing Association (secretary), Historical Diving Society (chairman), and International Divers Alert Network (chairman).

DESTINATION

39

IF YOU GO

➤ **Getting There**: Tobermory is roughly 190 miles from Toronto and 270 miles from Detroit, both of which are served by most major carriers.

➤ **Best Time to Visit**: The diving season around Tobermory runs from May to October.

➤ **Accommodations**: The Tobermory Chamber of Commerce Website (www.tobermory. org) lists lodgings options for the region.

➤ **Dive Shops/Guides**: There are several dive shops that lead trips around Tobermory, including Diver's Den (519-596-2363; www.diversden.ca) and G+S Watersports (519-596-2200; www.gswatersports.com).

DESTINATION

39

PALAU

RECOMMENDED BY **Wayne Hasson**

When asked to sum up the diving draw of Palau, Wayne Hasson was to the point: "On one dive, you can see almost everything that swims in the western Pacific. There's so much soft coral and deep water, just about anything can happen."

The Republic of Palau consists of 200-plus islands, on the southern edge of the Philippine Sea, roughly 600 miles east of the Philippines and 400 miles north of Irian Jaya (New Guinea). North to south, the islands comprising Palau stretch 400 miles, and are for the most part contiguous on a single barrier reef. Palau is one of the world's youngest independent nations, having established its sovereignty in 1994 after bouncing from Spanish to German to Japanese rule. Most of Palau's 20,000 residents live on four islands—Koror, Angaur, Badeldaob, and Peleliu. Diving is concentrated around the southern half of the archipelago and the Rock Islands (sometimes known as the Floating Garden Islands), which are the picture of tropical beauty, with requisite white sand beaches and swaying palm trees. Below the surface, a constant supply of reefs and walls, more than 1,300 species of fish—and a handful of wrecks—provide steady stimulation. "Most of the reefs at Palau reach right up to the surface," Wayne added. "You never need to dive more than a hundred feet, and you never have to fight against the current. You only need to dive fifty feet to take in the shark circus at Blue Corner."

Blue Corner is the site that perhaps best defines the Palau experience; it also happens to be Wayne's favorite spot. "I could dive that one dive every day for a week, four or five times a day, and it would be different every time," he said. "It's a magical place where everything seems to eventually pass by, going up or down the reef with the tides." Blue Corner juts out from the reef, beginning in shallow water and dropping off precipitously into blue water. The corner helps create the current that brings sea life by. Divers will generally

begin drifting with the current until they come upon a concentration of sea life; then they'll hook in on some rocks along the reef to take in the show. "I love diving with schooling barracuda, big schools of snapper and horse-eyed jacks, and gigantic Napoleon wrasse, all passing by with the tide," Wayne continued. "I've seen fifty sharks—gray-reefs and white-tips—suspended in the blue water; they're not eating, but they're probably thinking about it. When you do get to see them feed, it's quite a treat. They work together, circling around like an army to trap fish up against the reef, or they bust into a school to get their bite of the day. Sometimes you get so close, you can see their eyes roll back in their head as they watch you while swimming by. It gets your heart going. People don't generally get bitten by sharks, but it's occurred to me that if you were to get bitten, you'd want the animal to look you in the eye before doing it."

The Napoleon wrasse (also known as humphead or Maori wrasse) is a favorite fish for many visitors to Palau, thanks to its approachability and large size; some reach well over six feet and 300 pounds. "In my opinion, the Napoleon wrasse has more personality than anything else that lives in the water column," Wayne continued. "They're a big, jowly green creature, remarkably friendly. This is in part because divemasters at the Blue Corner would feed them hard-boiled eggs. They wouldn't have to even show the wrasse the egg, they would go for the pocket where the egg was resting. When the egg was presented, the wrasse would take it in its mouth, strip off the shell, and spit it out. If they figure out that you've got something to eat, they'll stick right next to you; you can't pry them away." (The practice of offering wrasse hard-boiled eggs has been discouraged, as poultry products are not typically part of the fish's diet.)

While day dives are available from the island of Koror, enthusiasts will get the greatest exposure to Palau on a live-aboard. The regimen on the *Palau Aggressor* goes like this: "You'll get up around six-thirty, have a sweet roll and coffee or full sit-down breakfast. By eight A.M., you're off in the tender boat, about to begin your first dive. After an hour below, you're back to the boat, where fresh-baked goods await. Guests have an hour or two topside to work at the camera table or recline in a hammock. By eleven, you're on your second dive; lunch is served at twelve-thirty. By two-thirty, you're diving again. When you return, hors d'oeuvres are waiting. There's another dive at five P.M., dinner at seven, and, if anyone wishes, a night dive. We save dessert for anyone who wants a treat after their evening dive."

There are a number of celebrated sites—German Channel, Big Dropoff, Shark City, and Turtle Cove, to name a few—that divers will want to visit. One Palau attraction that's a

OPPOSITE
No visit to Palau is complete without a visit to Jellyfish Lake, where non-stinging jellies have evolved.

DESTINATION

40

bit away from the reef is known as Jellyfish Lake, on the island of Ali-Malik. There are some sixty saltwater lakes among the Rock Islands; some have a tidal flow, some receive water through cracks in the islands' limestone strata. Eons ago, moon and mestiga jellyfish were separated from the open water and trapped in the lake. As these jellies face no predators in their sanctuary, they've evolved to the point where they no longer have the ability to sting—and they have multiplied into the millions. After a steep but brief climb up a forested trail, you'll come out upon the brilliant blue lake, and its ethereal denizens, flitting just below the surface. No trip to Palau is quite complete without a few hours snorkeling Jellyfish Lake.

WAYNE HASSON has probably spent more time underwater than above. An avid diver since 1967, Wayne began his love affair with the sea during an eight-year stint in the marines, where he certified scores of his fellow warriors and their family members. After departing the Marine Corps in 1978, he immediately began to furrow a deep trough in the dive world. Hasson founded the *Aggressor* fleet in 1984 and captained the first Cayman *Aggressor*. His approach to the luxury live-aboard concept has literally changed the way we explore the world. Today there are twelve *Aggressor*-franchised live-aboards. While in the Cayman Islands, Wayne helped install the first 112 permanent moorings and took the concept and idea to Belize, Turks and Caicos, the Bay Islands, Kona, and Truk. He also invented SASY (Supplied Air Snorkeling for Youth). Wayne founded Oceans for Youth, a program of marine science, diving, and awareness, to inspire the next generation of divers. Along the way, Wayne has accumulated more than 10,000 dives, and his award-winning photography has been featured in publications worldwide.

IF YOU GO

➤ **Getting There**: Travelers from the western U.S. reach Palau via Guam and Manila. Service is offered by Continental and Continental Micronesia (800-231-0856; www.continental.com).

➤ **Best Time to Visit**: You can dive Palau year round, though you'll find dryer weather in early spring and wetter weather from May through September.

➤ **Accommodations**: There are several live-aboards serving Palau, including the *Palau Aggressor* (877-348-2628; www.aggressor.com), the *Big Blue Explorer* (877-417-6160; www. palauscuba.com), and *Ocean Hunter* (+680-488-2637; www.oceanhunter.com). If you choose to stay on shore, accommodations are highlighted at www.visit-palau.com.

➤ **Dive Shops/Guides**: Dive Palau (+680-488-3548; www.palaudive.com) and Fish'n'Fins (+680-488-2637; www.fishnfins.com) both offer day trips.

MILNE BAY

RECOMMENDED BY **Stan Waterman**

"Earning my living as an underwater film maker, I found that working with big and poten-
tially dangerous marine animals provided a ready market," began Stan Waterman. "I focused
on sharks, and this allowed me to put my kids through college. While I was initially spurred
on by the romance of these big animals, I began to move on. I became interested in looking for smaller, more prolific targets for my camera. This has evolved into a fascination with
macro life and what's become known as muck diving. Milne Bay, off Papua New Guinea, is
one of the apex sites for seeking macro creatures."

The nation of Papua New Guinea comprises the eastern half of New Guinea, a landmass northeast of Australia. Reference books often characterize New Guinea as the second-
largest island in the world although thanks to its size, cultural diversity, and biodiversity,
many who know it well bristle at this factoid and think of New Guinea as a continent unto
itself. Papua New Guinea—an area slightly larger than California—has more than 850 indigenous languages, with most of its citizens living close to the land. (Contrary to tabloid per-
ceptions, the majority of social groups here are not cannibalistic; the last recorded incident
of cannibalism occurred in the early 1970s, and even in earlier times, the cannibalism was
limited to just a few tribes.) Papua New Guinea boasts one of the world's greatest levels of
biodiversity, and is home to 5 to 10 percent of the total species on the planet, many of which
are endemic. A quick statistic puts the breadth of Papua New Guinea's aquatic diversity in
perspective—it has twice as many marine species as the waters of the Red Sea and ten times
as many as the Caribbean! Milne Bay, off the nation's southeasternmost tip, lies at the inter-
section of the Solomon and Coral seas, and is perhaps PNG's greatest marine treasure.

"I was introduced to muck diving at Milne Bay," Stan continued. "I'd heard about the
experience and sought out Bob and Dinah Halstead, who were dive pioneers around Papua

OPPOSITE

*A seal with
a moustache?
Or a black-spotted
puffer being
cleaned by a
Pacific cleaner
shrimp? In the
muck of Milne
Bay, truly bizarre
creatures await.*

DESTINATION

41

New Guinea and coined the term 'muck diving' in the early eighties. It was incredibly eye opening. Every dive held a surprise, thanks to the big range of macro life present. I came upon fifteen species of nudibranchs, and wonderful poisonous creatures like stonefish, scorpion fish, and stargazers. I never saw anything like this assemblage of animals." The variety of critters is both amazing and expansive, and includes panda clownfish, twinspot, wunderpus, harlequin, ghost pipefish, spiny devilfish, cockatoo wasp fish, and Merlet's scorpion fish—for starters! That these creatures are a foot in length or less hardly diminishes their stature. "Some of the consumer cameras on the market today—both still and Sony video—allow you to fill the frame with the head of a shrimp," Stan added. "A miniature lionfish is just as exciting as an animal hundreds of times its size when it fills the frame. The optics now available enable you to shoot macro by lying quietly, waiting for the animal to come up—either on its own, or encouraged by a guide."

Though Milne Bay and Papua New Guinea are still very much on the diving frontier, there are some established muck spots that your divemaster is likely to show you. One is Dinah's Beach, a site on the north coast of Milne Bay. (While it is here that muck diving was "discovered" by Bob and Dinah Halstead, the name stems from the fact that Dinah's family—long-time residents of Papua New Guinea—actually own the beach.) Like other notable muck sites, the bottom here is not especially inviting at first glance; there are rotting tree trunks, coral rubble, and other detritus. But a closer look reveals a panoply of critters—five species of lionfish, blue ribbon eels, mantis and cleaner shrimp, six species of anemone fish, a host of nudibranchs, flamboyant cuttlefish, cockatoo waspfish, and Bugs Bunny scorpion fish. Better yet, all of these animals are in water that seldom exceeds thirty feet in depth. Nearby Observation Point is another famed muck-diving site, with many of the same characters present at Dinah's Beach, plus black crocodile fish, decorator crabs, and mimic octopi, among many others.

Though the muck may have put Milne Bay on the collective diving map, there is a wealth of other opportunities available. There are sensational reef dives, including Deacon's Reef (near Dinah's Beach), where enormous coral towers rise from the sea floor, and are interspersed with stands of staghorn, lettuce corals, and fan corals in all the colors of the spectrum. If pelagics are of interest, you might visit Giants at Home, a reliable manta cleaning station in just twenty-five feet of water. There are places to see hammerheads, places to see whale sharks, and sometimes even killer whales will make an appearance. For wreck enthusiasts, there are the intact remains of a P38 Lightning fighter bomber and a B-17 bomber of World War II vintage. And for everyone, there are opportunities to spend a little time on shore to gain some perspective on the cultural heritage of this fascinating land.

STAN WATERMAN has been at the forefront of scuba diving since its inception as a recreational sport. Between 1954 and 1958 he operated a dive business in the Bahamas with a boat he had built especially for diving. His first 16mm film on diving was produced during those years. For the next fifteen years, Stan continued to record his worldwide journeys and exploits on film; most were ultimately purchased as television documentaries. In 1968 he collaborated with Peter Gimbel on the classic shark film *Blue Water, White Death*. He was codirector of underwater photography and second unit in the production of *The Deep*, based on Peter Benchley's best-selling novel. In other collaborations with his close friend and neighbor Mr. Benchley, Stan was responsible for ten years' worth of productions for ABC's *American Sportsman* show. More recent productions include documentaries for ABC's *Spirit of Adventure* series and ESPN's *Expedition Earth* series. Stan has received numerous honors and awards for his work, including five Emmys, two gold medals from the U.K. Underwater Film Festival, four Golden Eagles, a Lifetime Achievement Award from the Miami Expo and from Boston Sea Rovers, the Cousteau Diver of the Year Award, the Richard Hopper Day Memorial Medal from the Philadelphia Academy of Natural Sciences, the Reaching Out Award from the Diving Equipment and Marketing Association, and has been named to the International Scuba Diving Hall of Fame. He is married and the father of two sons and a daughter, each of whom has acquired a special love of the sea from him. Stan and his eldest son, Gordy, a successful cameraman in his own right, won the first father-and-son Emmy for their work together in the National Geographic Explorer production *Dancing with Stingrays*. His first book, *Sea Salt*, was published in 2005 and is in its second printing. Stan continues to dive, film, lecture, and host dive tours.

IF YOU GO

➤ **Getting There**: Alotau is the departure point for most tours of Milne Bay. It's serviced by Air Niugini (+67 5-327-3780; www.airniugini.com.pg) from Port Moresby, PNG. Port Moresby has service from Brisbane, Australia, on Air Niugini and Qantas (800-227-4341; www.qantas.com.au).

➤ **Best Time to Visit**: You can dive Milne Bay year round. Visibility is highest June through October; November through May, different macro creatures show up.

➤ **Accommodations**: Most divers visiting Milne Bay will opt for a live-aboard, and Bob Halstead's Telita Dive Adventures (+67 5-3211-860; www.telitacruises.com) is highly regarded. Resort-based diving is available from Tawali Resort (800-684-9480; www. tawali.com).

DESTINATION

41

MALAPASCUA ISLAND

RECOMMENDED BY **Andrea Agarwal**

Andrea Agarwal's first dive at Malapascua remains one of the most memorable dives of her life. "I had heard about the thresher sharks of Malapascua and wanted to see them for myself," she began. "My husband, Trevor, and I were traveling in the Philippines, and we set aside a few days to visit the island. As we set out toward Monad Shoal, the adrenaline built up. We descended to a flat bottom as the sun was rising. We swam around for a few minutes, and then, out of the darkness, the silhouette of a thresher appeared, its huge scythe-like tail swishing gracefully behind. It swam closer and closer, and soon it was within a few meters. Its silver body glistened in the early morning light, and its distinctive tail, almost half its body length, followed lazily behind. The shark circled several times and then swam off into the blue. Before the dive was done, I had my first manta ray sighting. Wow!"

That two-day visit, by the way, has turned into five years and counting.

The Philippines are an underutilized diving asset for the American population, though there are certainly a number of world-class venues worthy of notice. Among the 7,000 islands that make up the nation, notable dive destinations include Tubattaha Reef, Balicasag Island, Anilao, Puerto Galera—and Malapascua Island. Malapascua is a small island a few miles off the northern tip of the province of Cebu, in the Visayan Sea. The name—which translates from Spanish as "Bad Christmas"—speaks to the island's European discovery on a stormy December twenty-fifth in the late 1500s. Blessed with beautiful white sand beaches, Malapascua has quietly catered to vacationers for some years, though it appeared on the diving map more recently, in the early 1990s. Its initial dive reputation rested on the daily thresher shark sightings it consistently delivered.

Thresher sharks are members of the mackerel shark family; they can reach lengths of nearly twenty feet, though half of their length is taken up by their namesake tail. Relatively

DESTINATION

42

little is known about them, thanks to their predilection for deep water and their nocturnal habits. It is known that they eat squid and schooling fish like mackerel, and that they are able to gather their small prey into tighter concentrations by using their tails. Because of their seeming aversion to bright light, your best chance of encountering them is early in the morning. "If visitors want to see thresher sharks, we encourage an early departure—as early as five, certainly no later than seven A.M.," Andrea continued. "We go to a spot called Monad Shoal, which is a sunken island at a depth that ranges between sixty and eighty feet. The edges drop off to over 700 feet, and the threshers come out of the depths to visit the cleaning wrasse that call the shoal home for a nice grooming. When you're down there waiting for them, it's like you're on safari. We move slowly, as if we're stalking them. When we do see a shark, we stop and wait. If we remain still, the sharks will come so close that we'll almost be able to touch them. Many times there will be several animals, and they will circle you. I see people every morning after the early dive, and their faces are almost always lit up with the excitement of having seen a thresher shark."

Thresher sharks may be the initial attraction to Malapascua, but as one might expect given its location in the Visayan Sea, the locale holds many other appeals. "Gato Island, a marine reserve and sea-snake sanctuary, has a huge diversity of marine life," Andrea said. "We see banded sea snakes, cuttlefish (often while mating), nudibranchs, frogfish, moray eels, scorpion fish, big-mouthed mackerel, and many white-tip sharks. It's a great place to come upon pygmy sea horses, and there's a tunnel that goes right under the island. There's something for everyone! Lapus Lapus Island has spectacular coral formations in very pristine condition. We have some excellent wreck diving in the vicinity. The *Dona Marilyn*, a passenger ferry that sank in 1988, is a favorite. There are several species of large rays in residence, and there are places where accomplished wreck divers can enter the ship. We're coming upon more and more great muck diving sites as well. The little creatures you find at such places are so incredibly well camouflaged—you get a buzz from finding the animal, and another from watching its behavior."

A day's diving at Malapascua ends with a fitting bookend to the dawn thresher swim—a twilight romp with mandarin fish at a site called Lighthouse. "We've dubbed it the 'Randy Mandy' dive," Andrea explained, "as very frequently we're able to witness the mandarins' intricate mating rituals. We leave the docks about forty-five minutes before sunset, as the show doesn't begin until about twenty minutes before dark, and it's a short run to Lighthouse. The mandarin fish live in broken hard coral at Lighthouse. As it gets closer to

OPPOSITE
Malapascua made it on the destination map with the promise of consistent thresher shark sightings.

DESTINATION

42

dusk, small groups of females collect, and a male (which is slightly larger) approaches one or more of the females and dances around her. When the male finds a willing partner, they shimmy together for a few moments, then rise a few feet above the coral. There's a puff of eggs and sperm, and they sink back into the coral. Sometimes the male will have time to find another female or two before darkness descends."

ANDREA AGARWAL is co-owner of Thresher Shark Divers (www.malapascua-diving.com) in Malapascua. A native of England, she taught diving in Thailand and Honduras before starting a scuba-diving school in San Francisco, Andrea's Aquatics. Tiring of teaching in cold water, she and her husband, Trevor, left for the tropics in search of somewhere to open their next dive shop. Originally they came to Malapascua to see the thresher sharks, but they liked it so much they stayed.

IF YOU GO

➤ **Getting There**: The island of Cebu can be reached from Hong Kong, Singapore, and Manila through Cebu Pacific Air (www.cebupacificair.com). Manila is served by many major carriers. Dive shops/hotels in Malapascua can arrange transportation to the island.

➤ **Best Time to Visit**: Diving is available year round. High season is December to April; the rainiest months are May, June, and September, though fewer than ten days are lost each year to poor visibility from storms.

➤ **Accommodations**: A number of lodgings options are available in Malapascua, including the Cocobana (+63 32-437-1007), the Hippocampus (+63 32-437-1030; www.hippocampus-online.com); and the Sunsplash (+49 42-146-5521; www.malapascua.info).

➤ **Dive Shops/Guides**: Several dive shops operate on Malapascua, including Andrea's company Thresher Shark Divers (+63 917-625-4195; www.malapascua-diving.com) and Sea Explorers Philippines (+63 32-234-0248; www.sea-explorers.com).

SCAPA FLOW

RECOMMENDED BY **Kieran Hatton**

"The wreck diving scene is massive in the United Kingdom," Kieran Hatton began, "and if there's a mecca for UK wreck diving, it's the Scapa Flow. Scapa gives visitors a chance to interact with the golden age of shipping. You can get access to very intact wrecks in very accessible water. I don't think there's anywhere else in the world where you can dive with warships of this generation as easily as you can here."

Given the region's rich nautical history and natural beauty, it's no wonder that wreck diving aficionados consider a pilgrimage to the Orkney Islands and Scapa Flow a necessity. The Orkneys—an archipelago of seventy islands—lie just above the northern tip of the UK mainland, and straddle the North Atlantic to the west and the North Sea to the east. At the south/center point of the archipelago is the Scapa Flow, a large natural harbor formed by the islands of Mainland, Hoy, Graemsay, Burray, and South Ronaldsay. Encompassing 120 square miles of sheltered water, Scapa Flow has been used as an anchorage since Viking times; in more recent history, it served as a major base for the Royal Navy in both world wars. From here, British forces could control access to both the North Atlantic and North Sea.

The foundation for Scapa's future fame as a wreck diving destination was laid in 1918, when the Flow was selected as an internment site for the German high seas fleet following the armistice agreement of 1918. Late that year, Admiral Ludwig von Reuter led seventy-four ships (ten battleships, six battle cruisers, eight light cruisers, and fifty destroyers) into Scapa to wait out the final terms of peace. After waiting six months, with little information and no sense of a clear resolution, Admiral von Reuter quietly made plans to scuttle the fleet to prevent it from falling into the hands of the British forces. On June 21, the entire fleet was sunk. Of the seventy-four ships scuttled, twenty-two were immediately recovered, and another forty-five were raised through considerable salvage efforts between the wars. This left three battleships and four light cruisers on the bottom. The second stage of Scapa's wreck diving development came as aggressions escalated toward World War II. To protect the British fleet at Scapa, many passages to the anchorage were closed off by sinking various ships—these came to be known as the blockship wrecks. Despite these and other safeguards (such as boom nets across key eastern entrances to the Flow), a German submarine gained entry to the Flow, and the HMS *Royal Oak* was sunk; 833 lives were lost. To prevent this from happening again, a series of causeways was built across the eastern entrances to the harbor. These became known as Churchill Barriers; together, with the blockship wrecks, they constitute a second diver's attraction to Scapa Flow.

The remains of the seven craft from the German high seas fleet rest near the island of Cava, which is between the larger islands of Mainland and Hoy. Each of the three battleships—the *Markgraf, Kronprinz Wilhelm* and *König*— measures over 550 feet in length. "The sheer size of the battleships is incredibly impressive," Kieran continued. "You can sit down on the seabed and look up at the *Kronprinz Wilhelm's* twelve-inch diameter guns—the cruise missiles of their day. Teak decking still remains in place, and you can even see the steering column if you know where to look. The engine rooms of the *König* and her sisters can also be accessed by the more skilled, adventurous divers. It's also possible to inspect the engine room of the *König*.

"Of the light cruisers—the SMS *Karlsruhe,* SMS *Coln,* SMS *Dresden,* and the SMS *Brummer*—my favorite is the *Coln,* which is the most intact of the four. The bow is completely intact; when you have a day with good visibility, you can hang off the bow and really get a perspective on the scale of these ships, which measure nearly 500 feet. They don't build ships like that anymore! There's a profusion of sea life around the bow as well—sponges, anemones, and a huge variety of fish. Drifting along the length of the craft, you'll come upon where the anchor chains hang, a reminder that these ships were in harbor when they sank." Where the battleships rest at depths ranging from eighty to 150 feet, the cruisers are a bit shallower, at forty-five to 120 feet. The guns of the *Karlsruhe* and the intact stern of the *Dresden* are two other memorable attractions. Remants of the forty-five ships that were salvaged from Scapa Flow provide clues of varying clarity to the majesty of these craft. Of the unsalvaged metal, the four main turrets of the battle cruiser SMS *Bayern* are most recognizable for what they once were.

Kieran described an average diving day around Scapa Flow. "In the morning, we'll generally dive one of the battleships or light cruisers. They're a short boat run from Stromness. We'll head back to town for lunch and visit the Stromness Museum, which has many maritime artifacts from the German fleet. In the afternoon, we'll dive another of the big wrecks, or visit the blockships in Burra Sound or those at the Churchill Barriers." Favorite wrecks among the blockships include the *Tabarka*, the *Gobernador Bories*, and the *Doyle* at Burra Sound; and the *Cape Ortegal* (barrier number 2) and the *Gartshore* (barrier number 3).

There are many attractions above the water at Stromness and around the Orkneys in general. "You have some of the oldest human settlements in northern Europe here," Kieran added, "lots of pre–Iron Age history, standing stones, burial tombs. You can really see the Viking influence here. There's also world-famous bird watching." And when the day's diving is done, one can enjoy a wee dram of Scapa single-malt whisky.

KIERAN HATTON is a dive instructor with Scapa Scuba (www.scapascuba.co.uk) based in Stromness, Scotland. He has done more than 1,000 dives in Egpyt, Australia, Mexico, India, Thailand, and all around the United Kingdom.

IF YOU GO

➤ **Getting There**: The town of Stromness makes a good hub for Scapa Flow expeditions. Stromness is served with daily flights from Inverness, Edinburgh, and Aberdeen on British Airways (800-247-9297; www.britishairways.com).

➤ **Best Time to Visit**: The diving season is April through October. Visibility is best at either end of the season; water is warmer in the summer.

➤ **Accommodations**: The Stromness Hotel (+44 1856-850298; www.stromnesshotel.com) comes well recommended. The Visit Orkney Website (www.visitorkney.com) lists other lodging options.

➤ **Dive Shops/Guides**: Scapa Scuba (+44 1856-8511218; www.scapascuba.co.uk) is a local dive shop that leads trips to the wrecks of the Scapa Flow.

DESTINATION

43

MAHE

RECOMMENDED BY **Debbie Smith**

Divers are forever searching for the next paradise, the next Garden of Eden. Some—including Debbie Smith—believe they have found it in the Seychelles. "As you fly in to Mahe, you're taken with the beauty of the place, even more sumptuous than the glossy photos in the tourist brochures," Debbie began. "When you finally are able to get into that warm, clear water, you find the most diverse, rich, and beautiful underwater environment. Each site is very different from the next. You won't see a lot of big sharks around Mahe and the other inner islands, but there's enough big stuff to keep people interested."

The Seychelles is an archipelago of 115 islands scattered over 150,000 square miles in the Indian Ocean, roughly 1,000 miles off the coast of Kenya, and 600 miles north of Madagascar . . . which is to say, not particularly close to anywhere. Far from any mainland and riding the equator, the Seychelles present as idyllic a tropical environment as one might imagine. The air temperature hovers around 85 degrees the year round; the water temperature is the same. The water is incredibly clear, and its turquoise tones are offset by the white, white sand and swaying palm trees.

The Seychelles's physical isolation explains why the islands went undiscovered until the early 1500s, when Portuguese explorers briefly landed here (it's believed that Arab traders may have landed here previous to the Portuguese visit, though no documentation exists verifying this). Aside from occasional stops by ships looking to harvest turtle meat, no settlement occurred here until the mid-1700s, when the French established some control over the islands; they were named for the French finance minister at the time, Jean Moreau de Séchelles. Over the next fifty years, England wrangled with France for control of the islands, finally gaining possession in 1814. In 1976, the Republic of Seychelles gained its independence. Historically, the islands' inhabitants relied on cotton cultivation, whaling, coconut

OPPOSITE
While shallow
regions suffered
some coral
degradation
during the
El Niño of 1998,
reefs in deeper
waters suffered
little damage.

DESTINATION

44

193

plantations, and the export of guano for economic sustenance. Since gaining independence, the government has set aside nearly half of the total area of the islands as nature reserve or parks, recognizing both the inherent value of these resources and their potential for tourism. The government, working with various conservation organizations, has also acted aggressively to protect the many unique species that call the islands home.

Debbie got acquainted with the diving possibilities of the island of Mahe—home of the nation's capital, Victoria, and most of its population—and those of surrounding islands, doing set-up work for North Island Resort. "It was a very different experience," she continued, "as most of my early diving around Mahe was very exploratory in nature. I didn't know where I was going half the time. I found a lot of good spots with the help of local fishermen. I offered them juice in exchange for information about reefs that were good fish producers. It was very rewarding to pioneer so many dive sites."

The shallower regions around Mahe suffered some coral degradation during the El Niño of 1998 when the waters heated to intolerable levels, but research shows that they are bouncing back strongly—and reefs in deeper waters suffered little damage. Thanks to the granitic composition of Mahe and the inner islands, the Seychelles's fish life has suffered very little. "At almost any of the dive sites you might visit around Mahe or North Island," Debbie continued, "you'll come upon a vast assortment of species. These include trumpet fish, bat fish, sweepers, octopus, paper fish, raggy scorpion fish, stone fish, emperor angel fish, all the members of the kingfish family, great barracuda, rock mover wrasse, huge shoals of fusiliers, white-tip reef sharks, and hawksbill and green turtles. You'll also get some pelagics like dorado, a variety of rays, wahoo, and even yellowfin tuna. We also have whale sharks present year round, especially between Mahe and the island of Praslin to the northeast. Sometimes you'll see five or six in one area; they can be spotted from helicopters. Many of the dives are quite shallow, perfect for beginners. But there are also deeper descents for more experienced divers." Thanks to its relative abundance of whale sharks, the area around Mahe has been the subject of ongoing whale-shark research conducted by the Shark Research Institute Seychelles and Marine Conservation Society Seychelles.

There are scores and scores of dive sites around Mahe and the inner islands. Dive centers on Mahe offer daily scheduled dives; if you opt to stay at one of the resort properties, you can dive whenever you wish. When asked to share a few highly regarded sites, Debbie mentioned Shark Bank, the *Ennerdale* wreck, and South Marianne off Marianne Island. Shark Bank is a series of submerged granite rocks in Beau Vallon Bay; home to gorgonian fan corals, it's a reliable spot to find large stingrays and sometimes whale sharks will come through. The *Ennerdale* was a 710-foot British oil tanker that ran aground in 1970 near Mamelles Island, north of Mahe. The ship's stern, including its immense bronze propeller, is largely intact, and the structure now attracts moray eels, groupers, eagle rays, lion fish, and large schools of fusiliers. At South Marianne, there are dramatic arches that often hold gray reef sharks, Napoleon wrasse, and eagle rays.

If you pass the island of Praslin en route to Marianne, you may wish to take a few hours to go ashore to visit the Vallée de Mai, a palm forest that continues to exist in a near-undisturbed state in a valley near the center of the island. The valley is home of the coco de mer palm, producer of the world's largest seed. The seed or nut of the coco de mer can reach weights of nearly fifty pounds, and contains two lobes; the shape of the lobes speaks to the plant's Latin name *Lodoicea callipyge*; *callipyge* is Greek for "beautiful buttocks." The seeds of the coco de mer attempt to expand their range through ocean dispersal. Until their source was discovered in the 1760s, some sailors believed that they grew on a magical tree on the ocean floor (presumably tended by mermaids with similarly well-appointed posteriors).

And some, incidentally, believe that the Vallée de Mai is the site of the biblical Garden of Eden.

DEBBIE SMITH's passion and dedication have led her into assisting top researchers in shark awareness and reef conservation. Since certification in 1986, she has achieved PADI Master Scuba Diver Trainer (MSDT) instructor status, and has been instrumental in setting up and establishing top dive centers at upmarket resorts in South Africa and the Seychelles, from mapping and naming sites to full operational status. These resorts have won top international awards. Debbie has written and had published articles on diving with great white sharks and is the founding member of an ecotourism company, Diving with Sharks (www.divingwithsharks.co.za). She was the first woman in Africa to be inducted into the Women Divers Hall of Fame in 2007 in recognition of her outstanding achievements as a woman in diving in the field of education, safety, research and conservation. Debbie has gone on to set up and head yet another company Africa Dive Expeditions, which is a dive/research operation, placing emphasis on education and shark research as well as adventure trips.

DESTINATION

44

IF YOU GO

➤ **Getting There**: Mahe, the principal island of the Seychelles, is served with flights from various European gateway cities via Air Seychelles, British Airways, and KLM/Kenya Airways.

➤ **Best Time to Visit**: The water is warmest and visibility is best from late November to late May. However, you can dive the Seychelles year round.

➤ **Accommodations**: Seychelles Travel (+248 67-13-00; www.seychelles.travel/en) lists a variety of lodgings options on Mahe and surrounding islands. North Island Resort (+248 29-31-00; www.north-island.com) is one of the dive operations that Debbie helped establish.

➤ **Dive Shops/Guides**: Seychelles Travel (+248 67-13-00; www.seychelles.travel/en) also lists the many dive operators on Mahe.

ALIWAL SHOAL/WATERFALL BLUFF

RECOMMENDED BY **Simon Enderby** AND **Jason Isley**

Jason Isley likes Aliwal Shoal for sharks. Simon Enderby likes Waterfall Bluff for sardines …and all the creatures they can attract. Both enjoy these waters south of Durban for the adrenaline rush they're almost sure to provide.

Aliwal Shoal lies about three miles off the coast of the town of Umkomaas, thirty miles south of Durban, South Africa, in the Indian Ocean. The shoal itself is relatively small, roughly a mile by half a mile, but it's gained a worldwide reputation for attracting a variety of sharks. "You'll come upon hammerheads, silkies, bull sharks, and ragged-tooth sharks," Jason said. "You get tigers there, too. They get the most press, and that's one thing that brought the Scubazoo team to Aliwal."

To increase the odds of bringing big specimens in close, Jason and his team used chum. "You drift in the current with the bait," he continued, "and hope that you get close enough to the sharks to get good shots. On one occasion I was in the water with dive adventurer Monty Halls and a large tiger, and our boat was manned by less-experienced operators. The visibility wasn't great, but we could make out a large shadow cruising around us. Looking up, I realized that the boat operator had taken out the chumline, and had stopped adding bait. As the shark circled closer and closer, Monty and I realized that *we were the bait*. We didn't want to repeat that experience and that's why it is very important to use one of the operators with years of experience such as Mark Addison of Blue Wilderness. An unexpected surprise on that trip was a number of whale-shark encounters. Every day as we made our way through the swells to get back to the beach, we'd have up to nine whale sharks feeding along the coastline. Visibility was off because of the surf; we'd get so close, the sharks would almost bump us on the nose. We became very nonchalant about finding them."

Though they lack the tiger shark's modest potential for mayhem, ragged-tooth sharks— or "raggies," in local parlance—are certainly a highlight at Aliwal. Raggies have a truly jarring set of choppers, with long, sharp teeth set madly askew on the exterior of their mouths. Despite their menacing appearance, raggies pose little danger to divers. When they're present in great numbers (generally from July through October, when it's believed that they use Aliwal as mating grounds), one can often come upon them in a resting state in the daytime at sites like Cathedral or Raggie Cave, allowing you plenty of time to view this member of the mackerel-shark family.

Come May and June, the action shifts a little farther south to a place called Waterfall Bluff, during the annual Sardine Run, a phenomenon that's been likened to the Great Migration in the Serengeti for its incredible aggregation of animal life, and the frenzied activity that unfolds as predators close in on the baitfish from all angles. "It's unquestionably one of the highlights in the underwater photographer's or filmmaker's world, the pinnacle, the Everest, to get to one of those baitballs during the Sardine Run," Simon explained. "We went down on assignment for a National Geographic Channel production to make a show about a British photographer who was bitten by a shark there while filming a few years before. The sharks will swim through the baitball with their eyes closed, mouth open. By mistake, the photographer ended up in the middle of the baitball. Luckily he was flown out and survived. The focus of the show we were filming was to capture his return to the Sardine Run and getting back into the water with the sharks and other creatures."

The Sardine Run is largely unexplained. The sardines are generally found in the colder waters off Cape Horn in the Atlantic, but each May they follow the cold currents that flow south to north to the waters off the southern KwaZulu-Natal province, often coming close to shore and into shallow waters. Millions and millions of fish band closely together, seeking safety in numbers. Their sense of security is short lived as there's a seemingly endless list of predators waiting for a feast—gannets, dolphins, seals, and sharks, sharks, sharks. (Copper, dusky, and black-tip sharks are common visitors; great whites sometimes show up.) But the sardines and their hungry retinue don't always have the good manners to show up when spectators expect them.

"It doesn't always happen as predicted," Simon continued. "There were a number of film crews on hand hoping to get footage, and we were the only production that had any real success that year. The baitballs are ephemeral—they can last ten or fifteen minutes, or just several minutes. The windows of opportunity are small. You need as many eyes out on the

OPPOSITE
Aliwal Shoal
attracts many
shark species,
including ragged
tooth sharks (or
"raggies"), with
their distinctive
dental work.

DESTINATION

45

ocean as possible, and the luck of being in the right place at the right time. We didn't encounter a baitball until the last day of our visit. Much of the credit for our good fortune goes to Mark Addison and Blue Wilderness Expeditions. Mark is one of the most experienced shark guys in South Africa, and our success is attributable to his logistical and local expertise.

"The experience goes something like this. You first push through six-to-eight-foot swells in Zodiacs to leave the beach and make open water. Then there's a lot of bobbing around. On the day we got our footage, we'd been traveling back and forth for hours before we saw gannets—thousands of them, it seemed—bombing the water like missiles. As we pulled closer, there were dolphins breaking the surface around the baitball, sharks, some fur seals—a mass of teeth and fish. The water was boiling like a cauldron, and there was the screeching of the gannets from above. As I was taking all this in, it went through my mind that I'd have to get into the middle of that fracas. We rolled off the side of the boat and my only thought was how to capture this amazing event on film. In front of me were thirty or forty dolphins whizzing around a hysterical ball of mercury (the sardines), gannets swimming past in an explosion of bubbles, sharks six to ten feet in length barreling through, coming up to inspect you, bouncing off you. Everything is happening so quickly, so manically, it's amazing how these birds, mammals, and fish work together without interfering with each other. How do the sharks miss the birds, the birds miss the dolphins? You can see the ball shrinking down, shrinking down, and the attack gets more frenzied as the ball gets smaller. Suddenly all the sardines—and all the other animals—are gone. The final scene is reminiscent of a snowdome paperweight—there are scales floating slowly down into the depth, and the shimmer of fish oil. It's my most incredible experience as a filmmaker; I'd do it again, and again, and again.

"The day I came back from the trip, I showed my wife some of the footage. She began hitting me about the head, upset with the risks she felt I had taken. But every time I think back to that dive, I smile and shake my head."

JASON ISLEY left the UK in 1995 to travel Southeast Asia and soon discovered scuba diving in Cairns, Australia. Having completed his PADI Divemaster, he then trained as an underwater cameraman and toward the end of 1996 joined Simon Christopher on Sipadan to help create Scubazoo (www.scubazoo.com). Scubazoo's filming trips have taken him around the world and he has now dived in Indonesia, Thailand, Philippines, Malaysia, Vietnam, India, Maldives, Australia, New Zealand, Tonga, Micronesia, Hawaii, Mexico, Panama, Canada,

Norway, South Africa, Mozambique, and Egypt. Jason has filmed on all of Scubazoo's major broadcast production projects. In 1999 he was one of the principal underwater cameramen in the world's first twenty-four-hour shoot in the Maldives, in 2001 and 2002 he managed all the underwater logistics and filming for the two UK *Survivor* series, and in 2002 was the supervising director for Scubazoo's role in the Canadian IMAX production *Sacred Planet* on Sipadan and in Thailand. More recently, Jason has been filming for BBC's *Really Wild Show* with Michaela Strachan, *Great Ocean Adventures* with Monty Halls, *Killer Shark Live* with Nick Baker, *Journeys of a Lifetime* with Minnie Driver, Animal Planet's *The Jeff Corwin Experience*, Nick Baker's *Weird Creatures* and *Perfect Predators* for Discovery's Shark Week. Jason is also an accomplished underwater photographer and his images have appeared in numerous books, magazines, and brochures; he was the driving force behind Scubazoo's first coffee-table book *Sipadan, Mabul, and Kapalai: Sabah's Underwater Treasure*, and more recently project managed their latest coffee-table book, *Reef*. He has done over 3,000 dives.

SIMON ENDERBY graduated from Aberdeen University with a B.Sc. (Hons.) degree in marine zoology. He was a leading figure in the first scientific research expedition to Pulau Layang Layang, Malaysia, in the South China Sea. Having worked with the Sea Mammal Research Unit and British Antarctic Survey in the UK, he returned to Malaysia in 1997 to survey the entire coast and coral reefs of Sabah and to run a turtle research program. Simon joined Scubazoo (www.scubazoo.com) in early 1998 and has been involved in many of Scubazoo's broadcast television filming projects. Simon assisted with the underwater logistics, planning, and filming of both UK *Survivor* series in 2001 and 2002 as well as project managing the Canadian IMAX production *Sacred Planet* on Sipadan in 2002. As underwater cameraman for Channel 5 UK and Animal Planet's *Great Ocean Adventures*, Simon has filmed extensively all over the world and racked up enough air miles to have flown round it more than six times. He has done more than 2,500 dives and is a qualified PADI & BSAC assistant instructor with TDI Nitrox, Extended Range, and Rebreather Diver certifications, as well as hard-hat and surface-supply diving experience. His dream is to retrace his ancestor's discovery of Enderby Land in Antarctica and compare their lives as old-school whalers to his life as a modern-day marine biologist/underwater cameraman.

DESTINATION

45

IF YOU GO

➤ **Getting There**: Umkomaas is the hub for trips to Aliwal, and is located thirty miles south of Durban in the KwaZulu-Natal province of South Africa. Durban is served from North America by several carriers, including South African Airways (www.flysaa.com) and United Airlines (800-864-8331; www.united.com).

➤ **Best Time to Visit**: For tiger sharks, January through May; for "raggies," July through October; for the Sardine Run, May and June.

➤ **Accommodations**: Umkomaas has ample lodgings options. On the high end, there's KwaMnandi Lodge (+27 39-973-1635; www.kwamnandi.co.za); a more modest option is Aliwal Dive Lodge (+27 39-973-2233; www.aliwalshoal.co.za).

➤ **Dive Shops/Guides**: There are a number of dive operators in Umkomaas. For the intricacies involved in diving with tigers or taking in the Sardine Run, Jason and Simon recommend Blue Water Expeditions (+27 13-973-2348; www.bluewilderness.co.za).

SHA'AB RUMI

RECOMMENDED BY **Dominique Sumian**

As chief diver on Jacques Cousteau's *Calypso*, Dominique Sumian had the opportunity to dive many of the world's finest reefs, long before they'd been "opened up" to recreational diving. After twenty-three years with the world's best-known and most beloved underwater adventurer, the place that stays with Dominique is Sha'ab Rumi, in the Red Sea off Sudan. "Shortly before my time with him, Jacques Cousteau did an experiment at Sha'ab Rumi—ConShelf II. I went back to the site at Sha'ab Rumi with Captain Cousteau three years later. I was struck by the density of the life there, and the clarity of the water. I dove along the wall that's near where the habitats were positioned, and the forests of coral were incredibly striking. There were many sharks present as well, including very large tiger sharks. I went back eleven years later with Philippe Cousteau, and it was exactly as beautiful as it was in 1967."

European divers have long understood the allure of the Red Sea, a body of water that offers a true tropical experience less than a day's plane ride away. Connected to the Arabian Sea and in turn the Indian Ocean (via the Gulf of Aden), the Red Sea stretches 1,200 miles, from the Sinai in the north to the small African nation of Djibouti in the south. It borders Egypt, Sudan, and Eritrea to the west, Saudi Arabia and Yemen to the east, and is 190 miles wide at its broadest point. The Red Sea is quite deep, reaching more than 8,000 feet in some places, but also boasts extensive coral reefs along its coastline. Thanks to the richness of its soft and hard corals and abundance of pelagic life—especially sharks—many Red Sea aficionados believe that the waters off Sudan provide the best dive opportunities. And along the 500 miles of coastal waters along this war-besieged nation, Sha'ab Rumi, twenty-five miles north of Port Sudan, is the best-known destination.

Sha'ab Rumi's notoriety comes in large part from the popularity of *Le Monde sans Soleil* (*World Without Sun*), Jacques Cousteau's second documentary film, and his second to win an Academy Award for Best Documentary Feature (1964). The film project grew out of Cousteau's desire to probe the possibilities of divers spending extended periods of time underwater. To Cousteau, having divers live underwater was the logical extension of the concept of saturation diving, put forth by a US Navy physiologist named George Bond—if a diver's body was saturated with nitrogen, the time necessary for decompression was already maximized. Hypothetically, this would allow the diver to stay below indefinitely so long as he was provided with enough air, food, etc.—and if the diver was able to maintain his sanity. In 1962, Cousteau and his team established Continental Shelf Station No. 1 (ConShelf I) in the Mediterranean Sea, at Pomègues. Here, two divers (Albert Falco and Claude Wesley) spent a week under water without major incident. Phase one completed, Cousteau began planning for ConShelf II. A site was selected—Sha'ab Rumi—thanks in part to its water clarity, abundance of sea life, and robust coral formations. This time around, five divers would spend a month below the surface. Their little village, at a depth of thirty-five feet, consisted of four main buildings and eight ancillary structures; the main building was dubbed Starfish House, and was complete with air conditioning and freshly cooked meals. (Additionally, two divers would spend a week at a depth of eighty-five feet.) Again, everything proceeded swimmingly. Among other things, Team Cousteau learned that in their oxygen-saturated environment, cuts healed much faster, and beards grew much slower.

The world learned that the reefs of Sha'ab Rumi were singularly beautiful. The Sha'ab Rumi site is divided up into several sectors—East and South. Sha'ab Rumi East is a ledge plateau and the actual site of the ConShelf II village. The shadows that are visible from the surface materialize into several structures, including the hangar for the team's two-man submarine and one of the shark cages that once formed a ring around the periphery of the village. Opportunities to brush against history aside, the eastern section of the reef is memorable for its stunning coral formations, a blend of hard and soft specimens in a dizzying variety of shapes and colors. Sha'ab Rumi South is equally venerated. It features a mini wall, with steep drop-offs to the east and west. The reef is festooned with a profusion of coral, providing a primer to the nearly 200 species that call the Red Sea home. Thanks to the steep drop-offs, many pelagics are drawn to the vicinity, including pick-handle barracuda, jacks, grouper, and humphead parrotfish; sometimes male parrots can be heard bumping heads. As the abandoned cages attest, Sha'ab Rumi South also draws a number of sharks, with gray reef, silver-tips, black-tips, and silky sharks being the most regular visitors. In the winter months, the reef can be one of the best spots in the Red Sea to come upon scalloped hammerheads.

DOMINIQUE SUMIAN was a critical participant in many Cousteau expeditions. Originally a commando marine and frogman in the French navy, he was dispatched to the French Oceanographic Service (COF) as chief diver and second captain on the SS *Espadon*, where he first served with Jacques Cousteau. Later the chief diver on the *Calypso*, Dominique researched and filmed in the Red Sea and in the Indian, Atlantic, and Pacific oceans. Among the films he worked on were Emmy-winners *The Sharks* and *Life and Death of the Coral Sea*, and award-winners *In Search of the Deep, The Whales,* and *The Unexpected Voyage of Pepito and Christobal*. He also worked with Philippe Cousteau as right-hand man and chief diver on many filming expeditions. In the intervening years, Dominique has created companies and managed others, with particular expertise in public relations and export and production management. He currently works for Aqualung, and serves on the board of directors of Earth Echo International.

IF YOU GO

➤ **Getting There**: Port Sudan, jumping-off point for Sudanese Red Sea expeditions, is generally reached from the west via Cairo, Egypt, with service from Sudan Airways (www.sudanair.com). Cairo is served by many major carriers.

➤ **Best Time to Visit**: Most live-aboards operate from October through June; the summers here can be unbearably hot for many (and unlike the ConShelf II team, you can't stay underwater the entirety of your visit).

➤ **Accommodations**: Sudanese diving (at Sha'ab Rumi and anywhere else) is conducted from live-aboards. Bookings for the dozen or so ships that operate here can be made through travel operators such as Tony Blackhurst Scuba (+44 14-8327-1765; www.scuba.co.uk) and Diving World (+44 20-7407-0019; www.divingworld.co.uk).

VAVA'U

RECOMMENDED BY **Paul Stone**

Many Westerners may not have heard of Tonga until it joined the coalition of the willing in the Iraq War in 2003 (sending forty-odd troops to the conflict), let alone been able to place it on the map. Situated in the South Pacific about two-thirds of the way between Hawaii and New Zealand, Tonga consists of 171 coral atolls and volcanic islands, clustered in three main groups—Tongatapu to the south, Ha'apai in the center, and Vava'u to the north. The Tongan people have a rich seafaring history; chieftains and explorers sailing out of Tonga from 1000 CE to 1200 CE created a loosely knit empire that eventually included much of Polynesia, including Fiji, Samoa, and parts of Micronesia and Melanesia. Despite their earlier proclivity for conquest, the Tongan people are known for their good nature. When Captain James Cook visited Tonga in the 1770s, he was so well received that he dubbed them "the Friendly Islands." (Even today, it is against Tongan custom to ever ask a guest to leave a home, and the national toast "*Ofatu*" translates as "I love you.") Tonga, it's worth noting, is the only Polynesian state to have maintained its independence throughout recorded history.

The hilly and richly wooded islands of Vava'u enjoy the majority of Tonga's tourist trade (though tourism is still a relatively undeveloped component of the economy), and provide excellent cruising grounds for sailors, including one of the best-protected harbors—Port of Refuge—in Polynesia. While Vava'u has been known for its summer cetacean visitors for some time (more on that later), divers are just beginning to understand the charms of its reefs and smaller creatures. "I'd worked quite a bit around the South Pacific," Paul Stone began, "and when I arrived in Tonga, I found that the water clarity was some of the best I'd ever seen. The reefs are also unbelievably healthy. I remember going to some famous venues and diving their showcase reefs; there'd be twenty yards of dead space, ten yards of good reef, another ten yards of dead space, and so on. Around Vava'u, we have reefs where you

OPPOSITE

Vava'u is gaining renown for the splendors of its reefs, but many still come for the chance to snorkel with the humpback whales that gather from mid-summer to fall.

DESTINATION

47

can go and go and go and there are no dead spots. I love small animals, and our reefs have some fascinating creatures—like Fiji, but perhaps even better. (In an earlier gig, I got written up for showing a client a nudibranch as a gray reef shark swam by; he was pointing at the shark, but I was more interested in the sea slug!) There are three places where we can find orange hairy ghost pipefish, a species discovered just a few years ago. Our giant clams are also of great interest to visitors."

Though Paul can overlook the passing gray reef shark to inspect interesting small critters, he can't refuse the call of the humpback whales, which call the sheltered waters around Vava'u home in the summer months. "For anyone who has any interest in nature or the underwater world, the humpbacks are mind boggling," Paul exclaimed. "If people have any passion for whales, they'll vividly remember every instance of every encounter with a humpback—if it's their first, their tenth, or their hundredth. I can't even count the number of times we've had 'been there/done that' kind of guys who act very matter-of-fact when they step on the boat. As soon as they see a whale up close, they freak out. We had a famous photographer on the boat last year to take some footage. After his first experience in the water, he came up after a three-minute encounter and realized that he'd forgotten to shoot any film. That's what happens when you find yourself swimming along with an animal the size of a city bus."

Humpback whales are members of the baleen-whale family. Adults generally range from forty to fifty feet in length and can weigh up to forty tons. Humpbacks feed on krill and will also take small schooling fish. These whales are renowned for their long migrations—some individuals have been recorded traveling as far as 15,000 miles from feeding to breeding grounds. Different populations of humpbacks have different migratory patterns. The whales that return to the waters of Tonga each summer—between 500 and 1,500 animals—migrate from the Southern Ocean below New Zealand and Australia.

"Vava'u, Tonga, is one of the two places in the world where humans can legally swim with whales," Paul explained. "The other is eighty-five miles off the coast of the Dominican Republic in the open sea. Many of the places where we'll interact with whales are very sheltered, which makes for a more intimate encounter. While some animals begin to show up in the spring, we think of the season beginning in mid-July. That's when the juveniles begin showing up. They seem eager to interact with the boat and with people. We've had many interactions when there are two to five whales circling us—I think they're trying to understand mating behavior. They're not mating with the boat, but displaying to it. From early

August through the end of the month, we observe heat runs. This is when you may have a dozen whales together, with one or two females in front, and a bunch of males chasing them. The surface behavior at this time is amazing. From mid-August through the end of September, mating-age females and males are starting to interact, and some calves are emerging. This is also the time when males are singing. When you have a male twenty feet or even eighty feet below you and he sings, you can feel the song going right through you. I can only equate it with the pulse, the throb that goes through your body when you're in the front row at a big rock concert and the band kicks into its first number. In October, it's mostly females and their calves. This is the holy grail, what touches people the most—to see an animal that's so physiologically different from humans display such tender maternal care. With a baby that's twelve feet long!"

Paul's wife and business partner, Karen Varndell, recalled an especially touching moment she shared with a mother and calf. "We spotted a mother and calf breaching in the distance, and we brought the boat up to within a hundred feet. They continued breaching and fin slapping, and then began circling the boat, first thirty feet away, and then just ten feet away. At that point, we went in the water—and the mother went to sleep. She was down below for about twenty minutes, and the calf was between us. She came up to get some air, and returned to her nap for another twenty minutes. This interaction went on for fifty-five minutes. I'm completely convinced that the mother felt comfortable napping because we were there to watch over her calf."

PAUL STONE is the co-owner of Dive Vava'u (www.divevavau.com) in Tonga. Originally from North Carolina, he has been in the dive industry for more than twelve years. Paul's diving career has taken him around the world, and included stints working in Truk Lagoon, Palau, French Polynesia, Belize, Cayman, and Indonesia, to name but a few. He is an instructor/trainer for TDI, and an instructor for a variety of other agencies, such as NAUI, IANTD, and SSI. After over 5,000 dives, Paul still loves the underwater world, and has a passion for underwater photography and videography.

DESTINATION

47

➤ **Getting There**: Several international airlines serve Tonga from Los Angeles, reaching the island of Tongatapu in the south via Fiji (Air Pacific) or Samoa (Air New Zealand). From Tongatapu, you'll need to fly to Vava'u via Peau Vava'u or Airlines Tonga to pick up your charter.

➤ **Best Time to Visit**: While good diving is available year round, the whales are reliably present from mid-July to October.

➤ **Accommodations**: The Tonga Visitors Bureau (www.tongaholiday.com) lists a variety of lodgings options on the island of Vava'u.

➤ **Dive Shops/Guides**: Vava'u has several dive shops that lead trips, including Dive Vava'u (+676 70492; www.divevavau.com).

GRAND CAYMAN

RECOMMENDED BY **Sergio Coni**

Corporate accountants, mutual fund managers, and banking executives know that the Caymans are a great place to conceal—uh, *conduct*—financial transactions. Divers know that the Caymans' greatest assets rest below the surface, and are inherently less complicated to interpret than the balance sheets maintained above!

"I came to Grand Cayman from Argentina twenty years ago to work as a dive instructor, planning to stay for a few years," Sergio Coni began. "I never left. While there are other places in the world where you will find more phenomenal creatures, there are several things that make the Caymans special. First, the water is extremely clear, clearer than the water at the hotel pool, and about as warm—78 degrees is the coolest, 86 the warmest. You can go to Bloody Bay Wall at Little Cayman and hover where the wall begins and feel like you're floating in nothingness. Second, the island of Grand Cayman provides all the amenities of the modern world, but you can get to very isolated, untouched places very quickly. Third, the Caymans in general give one the sense of being very far away from the day-to-day world, yet if you need to get back to the United States, you can do so in a couple of hours."

The Cayman Islands lie 150 miles south of Cuba (450 miles south of Florida), in the western Caribbean. First spied by Christopher Columbus in 1503, the Caymans attracted British interest in 1586 when Sir Francis Drake landed here. (Drake named the islands for the Carib word for saltwater crocodiles, which were once abundant here, though are now extinct.) The Caymans remain an overseas territory of Great Britain. They consist of Grand Cayman, where nearly all of the population resides, Little Cayman, and Cayman Brac. The three islands of the Caymans comprise the above-water ridge of the Cayman Trench, which plunges 8,000 feet off the islands' southern shores. While deeply plunging walls attract divers' attention, interesting underwater viewing can be found in as little as two or three feet

211

of water. "There are many places around Grand Cayman where people can snorkel, or even wade in the water and enjoy the marine life," Sergio continued. "One of my favorites is a place called South Sound, where there's a very shallow barrier reef and remains of an old wreck; the deepest spot is not more than six feet. You can swim across with a snorkel, or just stand up and watch, if you wish. You'll see eagle rays, nurse sharks, sea horses. I often recommend this spot to people who are unable to dive, as it's a great place to discover water creatures."

OPPOSITE

Feeding time at Stingray City, one of the cherished traditions of Grand Cayman diving.

There are more than 200 recognized dive sites around the Caymans; many are within easy reach of Georgetown, the islands' capital, and Seven Mile Beach, the hub of tourist activities. One of Sergio's favorites is Big Tunnels, which features a long wall with a steep drop-off and an impressive coral archway at the bottom (120 feet), which is often guarded by a school of tarpon. Another is Turtle Farm Reef, a shallower (fifty-to-sixty-foot) dive that gives visitors a "mini-wall" experience; it's adjacent to the Turtle Farm, which raises sea turtles and releases them into the wild. There are a number of accessible wreck dives, including the *Keith Tibbets*, a one-time Russian destroyer sunk for dive purposes near Cayman Brac. And there's the infamous Bloody Bay Wall on Little Cayman, where at a depth of twenty-five feet, the ocean floor plunges 6,000 feet; here, the panoply of corals and sponges that drape the wall is interspersed with myriad brightly colored reef fish. The deeper you dive, the more likely you are to encounter sharks, rays, and groupers passing by.

If you head out with a dive operator, odds are good that at least one of your days will end with one of the world's most highly publicized underwater experiences—a swim with the rays at Stingray City, a string of sand bars on Grand Cayman's North Sound. The story goes that stingrays started flocking to this location decades ago to feed on fish tidbits thrown overboard by local fishermen who were cleaning their catch. The sound of boat engines came to be associated with food, and the rays slowly acclimated to people, including those wearing tanks and bearing morsels in hand. Though it may not appeal to divers of all stripes, no one can deny the spectacle element of Stingray City. "The first time I visited the stingrays, I couldn't believe it was real," Sergio said. "I had been brought up being told that if you caught a stingray while fishing, you killed it; that they were mean. When you come and dive with them, you realize they're not dangerous. If you step on them, yes, you could get stung or scrape your foot on the rough skin at the top of their heads. But when you're swimming with them, they're very docile.

DESTINATION

48

"After Steve Irwin died, many people were scared of diving with the rays. They didn't seem to understand that he was working with a different kind of stingray, and that the chance of what happened is very remote. I describe it like this—if you're walking barefoot on a beach and step on a broken beer bottle, you wouldn't blame the bottle for your cut. In any case, interest in the rays has been picking up again. I dive with them almost every day."

Stingray City aside, one can't count on a lot of big-fish encounters at the Caymans. But with the islands' proximity to deep water, you never know what you might find. "Some years ago—in 1990—I took a group of divers to a site called Princess Penny's Wall, on the North Wall of Grand Cayman," Sergio recalled. "The group included a friend from Argentina. Conditions were excellent that day. Shortly into the dive, someone pulled on my arm and indicated they'd seen a shark. I looked down and could see something coming up from the deep blue. It was two hammerheads, and they came swimming right by us, checking the group out. I was a little nervous, but tried hard to maintain my composure, as I knew the guests were looking to me for guidance. As the hammerheads passed out of view, a school of four eagle rays came by from the opposite direction. The way the rays moved was as if they were in slow motion. It was a magic moment, and when we came out of the water into the boat, my friend and I hugged. I think we both felt as if we'd connected with these creatures.

"I just happened to see that friend recently in Spain. I was astounded at how many details from that dive—seventeen years in the past—that he still remembered."

SERGIO CONI is operations manager of Don Foster's Dive Cayman (www.donfosters.com) on Grand Cayman island. A native of Argentina, he has worked around the diving industry for over thirty years, including stints as a commercial diver in Argentina, before moving to Grand Cayman in 1988. Sergio has dived in Patagonia, Costa Rica, Venezuela, Bonaire, Margarita Island, Key Largo, California, and the Mediterranean Sea. He is married and has three children—the entire family dives.

IF YOU GO

➤ **Getting There**: Grand Cayman is served with direct flights from many eastern U.S. cities on a variety of airlines, including Continental, Delta, and Northwest. American Airlines and Cayman Airways (800 4-CAYMAN; www.caymanairways.com) offer frequent service from Miami.

➤ **Best Time to Visit**: Diving is very consistent throughout the year. Late fall through early spring tend to be drier and a bit less humid.

➤ **Accommodations**: The Caymans offer an extensive range of accommodations, from beachside hotels near St. George to secluded bungalows on Little Cayman. Cayman Islands Travel & Tourism (1-877-4CAYMAN; www.caymanislands.ky) lists options.

➤ **Dive Shops/Guides**: There are some forty dive shops operating on the Caymans. See an extensive list (including Sergio's operation, Don Foster's Dive Cayman) at www.cayman islands.ky.

DESTINATION

48

GRAND TURK

RECOMMENDED BY **Mitch Rolling**

There are few diving destinations around the world more associated with wall diving than Grand Turk. "People come to Grand Turk to dive the wall, plain and simple," Mitch Rolling began. "Clients return again and again to have an experience that doesn't vary much from visit to visit."

One can surmise that it's quite a good experience.

The Turks and Caicos Islands are made up of forty islands and cays, situated 550 miles southeast of Miami in the Atlantic Ocean, below the Bahamas and north of the Dominican Republic and Haiti. The Caicos Islands are farther west, slightly more developed, and contain the majority of the islands' landmass; the Turk Islands, Grand Turk and Salt Cay, are small and more laid-back. (Indeed, the donkeys, horses, and cattle that were used to haul salt during the heyday of Grand Turk's salt industry are given the right of way around Grand Turk.) The first Europeans to set eyes on the islands were the sailors under the command of Christopher Columbus, on the famous expedition of 1492. For the next four centuries, the fate of the Turks and Caicos mirrored that of many of the surrounding islands. Control bounced among the British, French, and Spanish, with the Brits eventually prevailing (Turks and Caicos remain part of the British Commonwealth). Many islanders were enslaved or died from disease. Relative prosperity (for colonists) arrived with salt raking, but the islands' arid climate made them ill suited for cotton or sugar cultivation, and colonialist interest waned—until the tourism potential of the island was recognized. The development of a Club Med in 1983 on the island of Providenciales signaled the islands' future.

On the whole, the Turks and Caicos Islands offer a variety of diving experiences. Around Providenciales (Provo), the focus is on the waters in and adjoining Princess Alexandra National Park; at Grand Turk, it's the wall. The Turks Island Passage separates the Turks

OPPOSITE

At Grand Turk, diving means one thing— "the wall."

217

DESTINATION

49

Islands from the Caicos Islands; it's twenty-two miles wide and averages a depth of 7,000 feet. The Grand Turk Wall adjoins the passage; depths plunge from thirty or forty feet to one and a half miles. Mitch laid out the wall's many logistical benefits. "First, it's situated on the leeward side of Grand Turk, so it's sheltered out of the wind and heavier weather. We lose very few diving days along the wall. Second, the wall begins just a quarter to a half mile from shore, and extends the seven-mile length of the island. The ride out to diving sites averages ten minutes. The visibility is excellent, averaging a hundred feet or more. Finally, since the reef begins at such a shallow depth it gets lots of ambient light, which both promotes growth and makes it easier for divers to appreciate the colors."

Dive sites extend along the western edge of Grand Turk, and are marked by mooring buoys. On an average day, Mitch will begin by leading guests to the northern end of the island. "There are three sites here I like—Aquarium, Rolling Hills, and Gorgonian Wall," he continued. "The soft coral here is extremely lush, and has excellent diversity—fans, plumes, and lace corals, a form of gorgonian coral. We'll then move south to some of the central dives. Here there are steeper drop-offs, and undercuts in the reef with black coral, which you generally can't find at recreational diving depths. It grows here because the overhangs block the ambient light. Overall, the reefs are incredibly healthy. As for fish life, I have definitely seen changes in the twenty-seven years that I've been here. I don't think we see as many bigger species, and the ones that we do see don't grow to the sizes that they once reached. Still, many visitors are excited to see 'so many groupers,' and it's great to hear that; everyone has a different baseline for comparisons. From May through November, manta rays are sometimes seen cruising the reefs, and even whale sharks will show up on occasion. Humpback whales migrate through the passage in the winter, and though we seldom see them while diving, we'll often hear them. Overall, I would not advertise Grand Turk as the place to see big animals, though certainly it can happen. The macro and invertebrate life, however, is quite rich thanks to the health of the reef."

It's safe to say that people come to Grand Turk as much for what's *not* there as for what's there. "Provo has a well cultivated tourist infrastructure," Mitch added. "It definitely offers some lovely opportunities, like the other more developed islands in the Caribbean. Grand Turk has wireless Internet and other modern amenities, but it's maintained the charms of a less developed place. The diving here is certainly excellent, but I think people come as much for the low-key experience Grand Turk offers. We head out at nine, do a couple of dives, and are back by one or one-thirty for lunch and beer and a nap. If guests want to do another dive, we'll skip the beers and go out again."

If visitors aren't too relaxed by nightfall, Mitch recommends a night dive at a site called the Library, which takes its name from the Victoria Public Library that rests opposite the reef on shore. "At night, there are generally less fish around, though invertebrate animals become very active," Mitch explained. "One of my favorite nocturnal creatures at the Library is the orange ball colymorph. It has a clear body with orange ball-like tissue at the end of its tentacles, and is quite exquisite."

MITCH ROLLING opened Blue Water Divers (www.grandturkscuba.com) in 1983 with one boat and an old compressor. Twenty-four years and 9,200 Grand Turk Wall dives later, Blue Water Divers has grown to include three boats and a complete retail dive shop, and is recognized as a PADI Gold Palm five-star resort. Mitch takes great pride in providing visitors with the right mix of professional safety and fun-loving camaraderie. When he's not leading dives, Mitch is an accomplished musician, and regularly gigs with his band on Grand Turk.

IF YOU GO

➤ **Getting There**: The island of Providenciales is served via Miami by American Airlines. Sky King (649-941-3136; www.skyking.tc) serves Grand Turk from Provo. The charter company Lynx Air (888-596-9247; www.lynxair.com) provides direct service from Ft. Lauderdale.

➤ **Best Time to Visit**: Diving is available year round at Grand Turk; Mitch prefers the summer months, when the water's warmer and there's little chance of fronts coming through.

➤ **Accommodations**: Turks and Caicos Tourist Board (866-413-8875; www.turksandcaicostourism.com) lists lodgings options on Grand Turk.

➤ **Dive Shops/Guides**: There are several dive shops on Grand Turk, including Blue Water Dives (649-946-2432; www.grandturkscuba.com). For a full listing, visit the Turks and Caicos Tourist Board Website (www.turksandcaicostourism.com).

PUGET SOUND

RECOMMENDED BY **Janna Nichols**

Janna Nichols had something a little different than Puget Sound in mind when she decided to take up diving. Something like Hawaii.

"At the time, my daughter was going to college in Hawaii," Janna began, "and I imagined that diving would be a great mother-and-daughter activity. My plan was to do my classroom and pool work here in Washington state, and then get certified in Hawaii. As I progressed in my classroom work, I realized that I enjoyed my instructor and fellow students. When they encouraged me to join them up in Puget Sound for our certification dives, I signed on. I got my certification in the cold water, and did eventually make it over to Hawaii. I really got hooked on diving there, but getting over frequently wasn't an option. That's when I began to understand all that Puget Sound had to offer. I haven't been back to the tropics for a few years now. The cold water we have doesn't bother me. After all, I'm a Pacific Northwest girl, and putting on some fleece is a regular habit."

Puget Sound is one of America's great urban diving grounds. Deposited between the Olympic Mountains to the west and the Cascades to the east, the sound encompasses nearly 2,800 square miles of water with an average depth of 450 feet, and stretches from the city of Olympia in the south to Port Townsend and Whidbey Island in the north. Much of Washington's population—some four million souls—live along or near Puget Sound. The sound is hardly pristine; the combined ports of Tacoma and Seattle are the second busiest in the country, and many heavy industries operate along its shores. Still, with the inflow from 10,000 creeks and rivers to dilute the effluents that reach the sound, and the strong push and pull from the Straits of San Juan de Fuca to inject nutrients into the system, Puget Sound supports a healthy population of marine life. While the visibility off Pike Place Market or Edmonds may not match that of Kona, one needn't see 150 feet to

OPPOSITE
Prehistoric looking
six gill sharks
are among the
largest fish you'll
encounter in
Puget Sound.

221

catch a glimpse of the resident creatures. In Puget Sound, the animals move a little slower.

"When you're diving in the tropics, it's fish, fish, fish," Janna continued. "You're almost overwhelmed by the vast numbers of incredibly colorful fish. People come to Puget Sound and ask, 'Are there *any* fish?' Well, we do have some fish. But the color comes from our invertebrates—anemones, starfish, octopus. Very large invertebrates. I teach courses in fish and invertebrate ID, and it seems that when I'm going through the list of species in class, we have lots of 'largest in the world' species." Of these "largest" species, the giant Pacific octopus is certainly king. "GPOs" can average sixteen feet in length from arm tip to arm tip, and weigh ninety pounds; the largest GPO recorded had an arm span of thirty feet and an estimated weight of 600 pounds! Capable of changing colors to foil predators or fool prey, GPOs have proven to be highly intelligent creatures, capable of quickly solving mazes.

Another large invertebrate associated with Puget Sound is the sunflower star. These giant stars can grow to over thirty inches in diameter, and can sprout up to twenty-four arms. They can move at lightning speeds (for starfish), up to several inches per minute, and have voracious appetites. "Sunflower stars are one of the apex predators of the Puget Sound substrate," Janna said. "They'll eat about anything that they can catch, including other starfish. I stopped to take a picture of one once, and suddenly another was crawling up my leg!"

There are more than seventy-five shore diving sites up and down Puget Sound, and hundreds more for those with access to a boat. The San Juan Islands, not far north of Puget Sound, open up a whole new set of opportunities. But Seattleites needn't wander far to find interesting underwater diversions—and it's possible to reach some after work. "A site that gets hit again and again is just across Elliot Bay and to the south in West Seattle," Janna said. "It's called Alki Beach. There are some artificial reefs there that attract a good representation of Puget Sound sea life. People like to night dive from a spot called Seacrest Cove Two. They're often looking for six-gill sharks, a fish that's generally found in much deeper water. When you come up from your dive, you're treated to the illuminated skyline of Seattle."

Another favorite site for Puget Sound regulars is Edmonds Underwater Park, heralded as America's first underwater city park. The park comprises twenty-seven marine acres near the Edmonds Ferry Terminal, and is home to many of Puget Sound's resident fish species, including lingcod, rockfish, cabezon, and wolf eels. Visitors owe a debt of gratitude to Bruce Higgins, who's volunteered some 25,000 hours of underwater labor over thirty years to make the park a safe and satisfying place to dive. Higgins (and more than 350 volunteers over the years) have added rope trails to lead divers through the park's highlights, and many structures to harbor animal life. He and his volunteers have been dubbed "The Egyptians" in playful recognition of their toil upon the sandy bottom of Puget Sound.

"When I started teaching the REEF invertebrate identification course," Janna said, "there was a set curriculum of forty-four species that I had to teach. I needed to take 'real-world' pictures of all of them, so people could indentify them. The first forty-three came easy, but the last—the Candy-striped shrimp—was more difficult. I understood that they frequented crimson anemones, which are more common in British Columbia. My husband and I went north and found countless crimson anemones—but not a single candy-striped shrimp. On the way home, we were going to pass Edmonds, so we decided to stop. We found a sunken boat that was covered with plumose anemones, and there among the plumose were a few candy-striped shrimp. That's the only time I've ever seen them."

Incidentally, the Edmonds Underwater Park has recently been renamed Bruce Higgins Underwater Trails; a small pyramid was recently erected on the bottom in Higgins's honor.

JANNA NICHOLS owns Pacific NW Scuba, which provides PADI-certified scuba classes, CPR and First Aid classes, REEF Fish ID classes, and DAN O2 training. She is a PADI master scuba diver trainer, DAN instructor, REEF instructor, and a dive safety officer with Washington State University. A member of the American Academy of Underwater Scientists, she regularly conducts REEF fish and invertebrate surveys, as well as participating in other scientific diving projects. Janna has championed efforts to identify and catalog invasive tunicates in Puget Sound. She's a passionate underwater photographer.

IF YOU GO

➤ **Getting There**: Most major carriers serve Sea-Tac Airport between Seattle and Tacoma. You'll want to rent a car, as many dive sites are easily accessed from shore.

➤ **Best Time to Visit**: September and October bring sunshine, slightly warmer water temperatures, and good visibility; hardy souls (with drysuits) can dive year round.

➤ **Accommodations**: The Seattle Convention and Visitors Bureau (206-461-5888; www.visitseattle.org) outlines lodgings options in the Greater Seattle area.

➤ **Dive Shops/Guides**: Two of the larger chains are Lighthouse Dive Centers (www.lighthousediving.com) and Underwater Sports (www.underwatersports.com).